Exhibit Design That Works

Praise for
Exhibit Design That Works

"Tired of wondering how to execute the perfect trade show experience? Wonder no more! This is the perfect handbook for exhibit theme and design. I wish I had access to it when I was a first-time exhibitor. Marlys takes a fresh and simple look at trade show exhibiting. Whether you are a first-time exhibitor or an industry pro, you will certainly find value within these pages."

~ Matt Wish, US Sales
Duo Display

"Are you looking for a quick read to get answers to your exhibit design questions? Then look no further. This book is easy to navigate and digest."

~ Elizabeth R. Besser
Former Convention Manager for BTC Exhibit Hall

"Since [trade shows] are expensive — it is beneficial to take the time BEFORE the show to get all your ducks in a row and be as effective as you can be with a plan of action and the research behind your actions — starting with this book."

~ Karin Roberts, Director of Marketing
The Tradeshow Network Marketing Group

"Some exhibitors think they can figure out exhibiting all by themselves. But why waste valuable time with a learning curve when you can learn from an expert?"

~ Bev Gray, President & CEO
Exhibit Edge

*"When I was new in the exhibits business my learning was accelerated by reading **Build a Better Trade Show Image** by Marlys Arnold. I was amazed how much information was in that book that applied to real world situations I was experiencing ... I'm expecting this book to further increase my understanding of what makes a great trade show booth and experience. I can only say do yourself a favor — after you read **Exhibit Design That Works**, read Marlys' other book, and take advantage of what is available in the Exhibit Marketers Café. Get to 'YES — Your Exhibit Success' with what she has to offer."*

~ Don Jalbert, President
Exhibit Associates Inc.

Exhibit Design That Works

Create a Trade Show Display that Gets Noticed & Gains Clients

Marlys K. Arnold

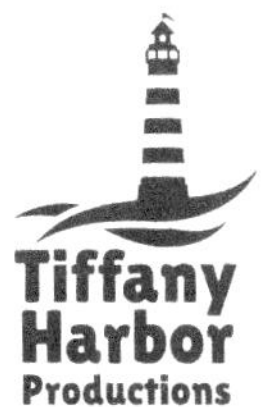

Tiffany Harbor Productions

Dedication

To my husband and biggest supporter, Alan: Thanks for coming along with me on the adventure of accomplishing our dreams!

To all my clients, past, present, and future, who allow me to assist in your exhibit marketing success: You challenge and inspire me. I hope this book does the same for you.

FREE: Exhibit Design That Works
Bonus Materials Online

Ideas are great, but they aren't nearly as valuable until you take action. So I've created a free site online which includes more in-depth resources to expand your learning, including downloadable checklists, bonus audio interviews, photos or links to case studies, and more.

If you really want to take the information in this book to the next level, you'll want access to these supplemental materials. They're organized by the same sections and chapters, so it's easy to find what goes along with what you're reading. And because there are always new case studies and resources, I'll continue to add those online as well. So be sure to bookmark the bonus materials link and check back occasionally to stay updated.

Here's the link for free access to all the bonus materials:
www.ExhibitMarketersCafe.com/designbonus

Contents

Part 5: Design with the End in Mind

Part 6: The Life Cycle of Exhibits

Foreword

I met Marlys when she conducted a class for new exhibit professionals. I've been fan ever since of her straightforward, helpful information about trade shows. As an exhibit designer for over a decade, I have learned that there's a distinct difference between exhibitors who understand trade show marketing and those who don't, particularly when it's time to get your hands dirty with the exhibit design process.

In the pages ahead, you will find an Exhibit Design 101 course that's perfect for exhibitors looking to improve the effectiveness of their trade show properties. Exhibitors should also consider learning the "designer lingo" described in the later chapters of the book. Mastering these introductory design terms will help you communicate clearly with the structural and graphic designers working on your exhibit. Speaking the same language saves time and avoids expensive misunderstandings.

It's also a great introductory book for trained designers — graphic, industrial, etc. — who are itching to design trade show exhibits. Whichever category you fall into, pay careful attention to the beginning chapters of the book. These chapters cover the foundation of any good exhibit design: Deciding on a core message to communicate and considering the attendees' perspective.

Since earning an MA in Exhibition Design, I've worked with countless exhibitors to create spaces that fit their needs, and I've followed the same guidelines Marlys describes in Chapters 1 and 5, "Keys to a Winning Theme" and "Speaking the

Attendees' Language." I can't be successful if I only meet the physical needs of overhead signage, eye-catching structures, storage, and meeting spaces.

There is always an underlying need to create a BRAND EXPERIENCE that visitors must feel on a subconscious, first-impression level. I love to ask my clients: "What do you want visitors to feel when they are in your space? What feeling do you want to reverberate when they have left your booth?" Those responses, usually a handful of adjectives, allow me to identify their emotional trade show goals. Some of my favorite real responses are opulent, badass, and sparkling! There are no wrong answers, and each brand is unique in the image it wants to project.

In other words, identifying your exhibiting goal and what will attract your audience should take place *before* you start planning the structural design. Everything else — structure, graphics, colors, materials, and giveaways — will follow once that foundation has been laid. And that leads to a cohesive and successful exhibit, not just at the show, but in Marlys' words, "It also makes your booth more memorable in the days and weeks that follow so the attendees are more likely to think of you when they are ready to buy."

Best of luck to you and much inspiration in all your future exhibit design endeavors!

~ Katina Rigall Zipay,
Creative Director,
Classic Exhibits

Introduction

Whether you're brand-new to exhibiting or you've been to more trade shows than you can count, odds are you haven't spent much time up until now focused on the strategy behind your exhibits. Most exhibitors are too caught up in crossing things off their checklist (Booth space reserved: Check! Graphics ordered: Check! Flights and hotel booked: Check!) to see how it all fits together.

In the **YES: Your Exhibit Success** series, we'll break down not only what you need to do, but also the thought process which needs to go into each step. And there's no better place to begin than with the design of your exhibit and the message it conveys.

Successful exhibitors design a booth that reflects their objectives for exhibiting and communicates their core message to attendees in a clear and compelling way that converts visitors into clients. It doesn't matter how much you spent on the structure — some inexpensive displays can be extremely effective. It's actually about how well you communicate the benefits of your product or service in a way visitors can't resist.

Let's face it ... with all the information available online today, it's more important than ever to deliver an experience in your booth that attendees can't get elsewhere. A static display of products really isn't all that different from your website, other than it's in 3-D.

Over my years as an exhibitor, show organizer, and now a trade show marketing consultant, I've seen a lot of bad exhibits. You know, the kind where the booth staff is embarrassed to be seen in it, or where they often hear "So what is it that you guys do?" from the attendees who actually do stop.

I can remember some of the ones that missed the mark by a wide margin: the giant brain on a spinning tower that everybody noticed, but nobody could figure out what it was for and it became the running joke of the show. Then there was the lifeguard up on a chair at the corner of a booth which didn't connect with what the company did and felt a little creepy. I could go on and on, but basically here are the signs of a bad exhibit to watch out for:

- It no longer represents what you do (or doesn't even use your current logo or graphics)
- The 'retro' look isn't in (or at least not your version of it)
- The display and/or graphics look shoddy and worn (or are simply poor quality)
- There's not enough space for the number of visitors – or even staff, for that matter
- It's too focused on splash and sizzle with too little attention to your core message and products (as in the examples above)
- It's not right for that audience (sometimes you need different looks for different shows)
- There's nothing to define who you are, what you do, and why attendees should care

In the chapters that follow — many of which began as posts on the **Trade Show Insights** blog — we'll cover how to overcome all of these issues and more. You'll discover how to develop a memorable theme, communicate your message in a way that connects with attendees, and design a multisensory experience. Then we'll break things down into the individual elements that define your exhibit: colors, graphics, materials, lighting, and more.

How to Use This Book

No matter your level of experience in the world of trade shows, this book has been designed with tools for you. It is organized into six sections that focus on the various aspects of designing an effective exhibit display.

You will also discover special elements to assist in your progress:

- **Trade Show Terms to Know:** When you come across a term you aren't familiar with, check this section in the back of the book.
- **What's Next?:** At the end of each of the six sections in the book, you'll find a few questions to jumpstart your planning process.
- **Resources:** Looking for someone to design/build your exhibit, or some other related resource? Check this list in the back of the book.

You won't find any photos in this book, but you can see photos (or even videos) of many of the examples online in the free bonus materials. Simply visit www.ExhibitMarketersCafe.com/designbonus to access all the additional resources.

I would also love to hear about any successful ideas you've used in your exhibiting, whether they were sparked by reading this book or not. Feel free to use the Contact page on www.TradeShowInsights.com to share your story and you may just find yourself featured on the blog or in a future book!

Although numerous resources are listed in the text and resource guide, you're not obligated to use any of them. Take some time to investigate your options before hiring any supplier.

Please note that I cannot answer every question related to the topics in this book. Due to the high volume of mail received, I may not be able to reply to every message.

~ Marlys Arnold

Part 1:
Develop a Memorable Theme

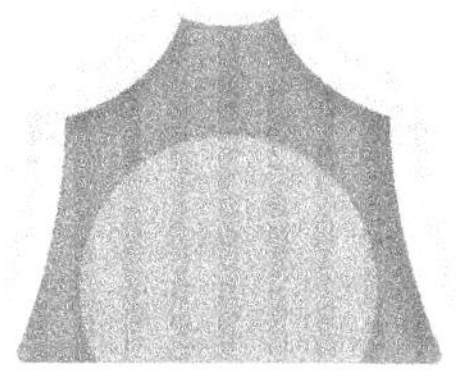

Ideas are a funny thing — they hit when you least expect them, yet can be incredibly illusive when you're on a deadline.

That could be partly because most exhibitors design backwards, starting with the physical elements of the exhibit (basic structure, fixtures, graphics, etc.) instead of beginning with the overall message they want to convey and the objectives they want to achieve.

So before you launch into designing your booth display, first define your basic message or theme. Often, this is an extension of your overall marketing campaign — don't think of exhibiting as a separate kind of marketing, think of it like a three-dimensional ad brought to life. And using a creative theme helps to define that 3-D message. It can also help to create a mood or atmosphere in your booth, creating an emotional connection with attendees — make them *feel* something!

Don't do a theme just to be cute!
When used as part of your
overall marketing plan, a theme
can really reinforce brand.
It also helps to distinguish
you from all the other exhibits.

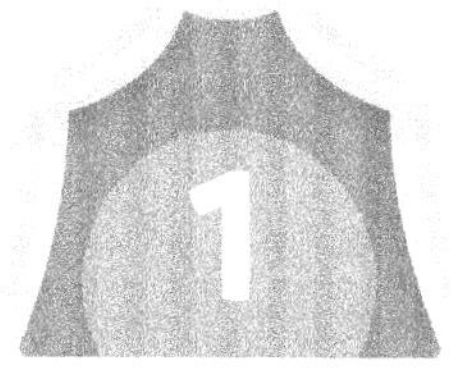

Keys to a Winning Theme

Using a theme helps to give your exhibit focus and make your message more memorable for attendees. To be most effective, it should be incorporated into all elements of your exhibit marketing, not just the display itself. Don't look for a gimmick — your theme needs to trigger an emotional response, reinforce your brand, and distinguish you from all the other exhibits on the show floor.

A great theme doesn't have to be expensive. In fact, some very clever and memorable exhibits have been done with very small budgets, as you'll discover in upcoming chapters.

Want to create a memorable theme for your next exhibit? Keep in mind the following tips and remember the whole point of a theme is to reinforce your message. Don't do a theme just to be cute! If attendees remember your great theme, but don't (or can't) associate it with your company and products or services, then you have failed. Here are some basic principles:

- Make it current — tie in with trends or events (i.e. be inspired by TV shows or movies)
- Avoid cliché or overused themes
- Be consistent with your corporate personality
- Align it with your products and/or services

- Play off the show's theme or location

- KISS ("Keep it smart and simple")

- Get your whole team involved in the planning process

- Hit an emotional nerve; play on attendees' memories of childhood or a great place

Remember: Define what impression you want visitors to leave your booth with and then design cues that will create that impression.

Steps to start creating your memorable theme:

- **Gather company brochures, product descriptions, catalogs, and any other marketing materials for reference.** Study those along with your current company ad campaigns and websites for recurring messages or themes that you can use as a starting point.

- **Ask current clients or customers to share what they like best about your product or company.** They may have some great insights you hadn't even considered.

- **Brainstorm with staff to boil your core message down to between three and five sentences, then pick one major concept.** Look for a metaphor you can build around that would convey that concept. (You'll see some examples of this in the next few chapters.)

- **Once you've decided on your core message, keep it consistent throughout all elements:** pre-show mailers, booth display, in-booth attractions, giveaways, follow-up materials, and more.

Just be sure whatever theme you're choosing makes sense and aligns with your company's overall message and objectives for exhibiting.

*(Portions of this chapter excerpted from **Build a Better Trade Show Image** © 2002 by Marlys Arnold.)*

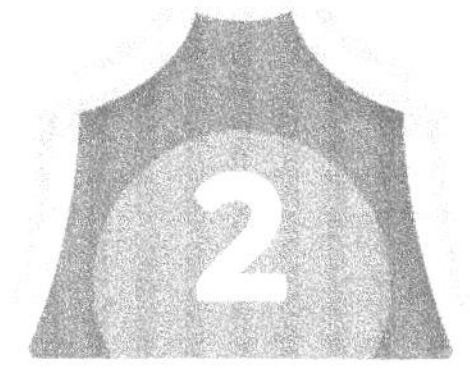

Theme Ideas to Build On

Exhibit theme ideas can come from anywhere: TV, movies, children's stories, travel locations ... the possibilities are endless! Not that all themes have to be cute or funny, but they should spark some kind of emotion in both you and your audience.

In a sea of same-old-same-old exhibits with predictable graphic backwalls or banners touting all the benefits of the exhibiting company, it often doesn't take much creativity to catch attendees' attention. Even if you're in a small space, you can implement a clever theme that will help make you more memorable instantly.

If you've read **Build a Better Trade Show Image**, you know the importance of experiential themes for exhibits. Using core concepts from the following examples of well-executed themes, think about how you could take a similar idea and build around it for your next show.

Recipe for Success

Everyone can relate to food, so it's no surprise that a food-related theme is not only popular, but also memorable.

I've seen this done in countless ways. One exhibitor sent out a pre-show mailer that looked like a refrigerator and included a scratch-and-sniff sample. They teamed up with a local culinary school to provide tasty demonstrations in the booth and also hosted a VIP event one evening after the show closed.

Another exhibitor hosted a celebrity chef in the booth who made desserts while attendees watched, then offered samples of her creations. Throughout her presentation, she tied the cooking analogy back in with key points about the exhibiting company with references like, "start with great ingredients" and "combine part technique, part creativity."

A twist on this is the farmer's market theme, where products are displayed on crates and barrels as if they were produce. This stands out especially well in a show that's geared toward high-tech products or something else that wouldn't be expected to be presented in that style.

I even used the food theme myself once to promote my book and consulting services. (This was before I launched the Exhibit Marketers Café online training site.) I set up a table with place settings on it, with the book laying on top of each plate as if it were the "main course." I designed a printed menu listing my products and services, then found menu covers at a local restaurant supply place. (There was also a smaller, "take-home" version for attendees.) My assistant and I wore blue aprons to coordinate with the book cover.

Just Relax

Another theme that translates well to many audiences and messages is one that creates a relaxing, zen-like feeling.

For example, one exhibitor who chose to promote the fact that clients can relax and let them take care of things created a spa-like environment with bamboo, foliage and water. The metal truss work was covered in green fabric, and a ceiling fan hung from the center of the booth. In one corner of the island booth space, a massage therapist provided brief chair massages. Giveaways included bottled water and wooden back massagers.

One year at the EXHIBITOR Show in Las Vegas (now known as EXHIBITOR*LIVE*), exhibit designer Classic Exhibits shared the message that working with them was "a walk in the park." So they created a peaceful oasis with a floor printed to look like grass with a walking path. There was also a fountain and swing set, with branding messages on the swings. No detail was overlooked … even the stairs to the second floor of the exhibit were wrapped with graphics of stepping stones.

Travel Back in Time

Retro or rustic themes can look fresh when done with the right pairing of color, graphics and props — think of a 1950s surf look or Route 66 design. Attendees are instantly transported in place and time.

YETI Coolers has a brand built around rugged and epic adventures, so creating a rustic display with the theme "Built for the Wild" was an ideal fit for them at the Outdoor Retailer (OR) show. Weathered wood, rusty barbed wire, and corrugated sheet metal set the stage in an exhibit designed by Roundhouse and built by Condit. There was a campfire conference area with a glowing faux fire inside a metal silo. A vintage truck bed hung on one wall, serving as a frame for a TV screen and of course one of YETI's classic coolers. The exhibit not only captured attendees' attention, but also won a "Best of Booth" award at the OR Winter Market 2017.

On the other hand, you wouldn't expect to see a wild west saloon at the Specialty Equipment Market Association (SEMA) show for the automotive industry. Yet that's exactly what PPG Automotive Refinish (a division of PPG Industries, Inc.) did one year with an exhibit designed by Lucarelli Designs & Displays, Inc. Named the Watering Hole, the rustic structure towered above the show floor in a desert setting complete with tumbleweeds. Inside the saloon, PPG water-based paints (thus the connection) were showcased on unexpected items like vinyl records, guitars, and cow skulls, while out front there were motorcycles and antique trucks painted in vivid colors.

Full-Service Theme

Lynch Exhibits used their booth to bring an ongoing ad campaign to life. The pre-show mailer featured artwork of a 40s-era service station and attendant. Prospects were invited to "Come behind the scenes to meet the high performance exhibit design and service team of Lynch Exhibits." The back flap was a "High Performance Exhibit Request" to be filled out and brought to the booth to indicate interest level – from a Tune-Up (hesitation in communicating your message) to a complete Overhaul (stop "blowing smoke"). Many of those who stopped by the booth either brought their card with them (pre-qualifying themselves) or at least remembered receiving it.

The booth itself was a total immersion in the theme. Built like a service station, complete with an old-fashioned pump out front (bearing the Lynch logo), the island booth definitely stood out. Staffers even dressed in the green attendant's uniform and hat. The giveaways also followed the theme — packaged inside an "oil can."

One more touch to the Lynch theme was a hospitality event held at the host hotel. Still following the 40s-era theme, it was billed as a Hometown Heroes celebration and featured a Congressional Medal of Honor Recipient. One wall featured a giant letter of hope, where attendees could write words of encouragement to troops overseas. And because the whole point of a hospitality event is to communicate your message in a low-key way, Lynch featured one of their products, the I-Wall slider (a sliding monitor which allows for self-exploration of information), to run a video profiling Medal of Honor recipients.

Un-booth

Exhibit Works took a very different approach with an "Un-booth" theme where "Un" stood for "unconventional, unexpected, and unforgettable." Using dandelion imagery, pre-show promotions set the stage with an invitation to sign up for an in-booth studio session to "plant the seeds of inspiration."

The booth attraction centered around a creative twist on a classic icon of childhood — the cootie catcher. Each attendee selected stickers (including some with scratch-and-sniff) to create their own design to take home, complete with a logo-branded display stand. (Mine is still on the shelf in my office!) Then instead of hosting a contest, Exhibit Works used the cootie catchers to determine a donation amount for the Suite Dreams Project, an organization dedicated to bringing comfort and joy to sick children.

Dandelions played a starring role in the booth, not only in the graphics, but also an innovative 3-D artwork suspended above the booth — made up of dozens of the cootie catchers! The plant-based theme continued through the follow-up, which included a seed packet.

More Ideas for Creative Themes

After walking countless show floors over the past two decades, I can tell you I've seen some very unusual themes, and I try to always document the ones worth sharing. So here are a few more that might spark your imagination.

- **"Our Company Wants You"** — A promotional marketing company played off both an election year and a show's location in D.C. with a pre-show mailer button sporting their own take on the classic Uncle Sam poster. Attendees wearing the button around the show floor received gifts, including teddy bears dressed in red or blue t-shirts and the classic white "campaign" hat with a red, white and blue striped ribbon on it. Instead of lead cards, the exhibitor used "ballots" to collect attendee information.

- **"In the Ballpark"** — Baseball creates a fun and memorable theme that lends itself to a variety of messages ("cover your bases," "knock it out of the park," etc.), whether for products or services. Create a mini-ballpark in the booth with turf instead of carpeting, plus a small set of bleachers in one corner for in-booth presentations with the staff wearing baseball jerseys.

- **"Slam Dunk"**— This theme appeals to basketball fans with staffers dressed like whistle-toting referees. Attendees can shoot baskets for a sports ticket giveaway.

- **"Story Time"** — Creating a colorful storybook or comic book look conveys your message in a fun and whimsical way that gets lots of attention on an otherwise bland show floor. (Plus having costumed characters involved makes for great attendee photo opportunities!) I've seen this done with everything from Alice in Wonderland to comic book superheroes created especially for that particular exhibiting company.

A good theme that is well thought out, combined with an all-encompassing experience can not only help you stand out in a sea of generic backwall displays, but can also help attendees remember you. And that's the whole point of being there!

Inside the bonus materials for this chapter:

- Photos and/or links to some of the case studies mentioned
- Links to Pinterest boards on exhibit design
- Videos of cool ideas from EXHIBITOR*LIVE*
- Periodic Table of Exhibit & Event Themes

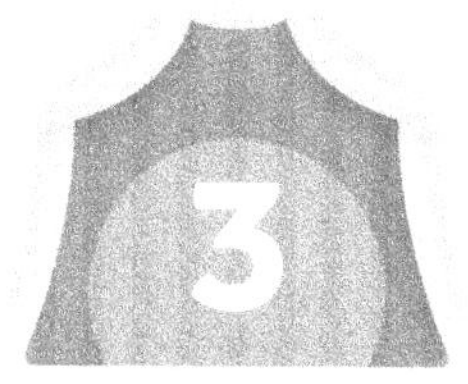

Small but Mighty

Bigger isn't always better. You don't need a huge island booth to pull off a great theme — some of the most clever ones can be accomplished in a 10-by-10-foot or 10-by-20-foot inline space! Here are a few to give you inspiration:

- **"Are You Being Served?"** — Exhibit designer Falcon Perspectives, Inc., created a retro diner. A menu board showcased their various services, and a bar area provided a place for attendees to sit and ask questions while sipping a bottled water or nibbling on something from the sweets jar. The Falcon staff also created an actual 'menu' as an in-booth brochure, which listed key ingredients, starters, and specials of the day. And they did it all in a 10-by-20-foot space!

- **Picnic** — I saw this done very well using a faux-grass backwall with a picnic table placed up next to it it for product displays.

- **"Doing More with Less"** — When the economy was bad, many exhibitors struggled trying to design a booth that walked the fine line between scaled-back and cutting-edge. Exhibit designer Kubik faced the subject head-on with a back-to-basics theme: "Cutting back shouldn't leave you feeling empty." Using baker's racks and a hand-lettered chalkboard backwall, they featured brown bag "snack packs" with fresh-baked cookies. Staff wore aprons that asked the question, "Feeling empty?" and the smell of cookies worked to attract attendees to stop. Follow-up e-mails reminded attendees to "be a smart cookie and contact us to do more with less."

- **DIY Design** — It never hurts to get the audience interacting with your exhibit design. I've seen this done well in a variety of ways. Some exhibitors have a question printed on a blank backwall with colorful markers on hand for attendees to write or sketch their ideas. This has an added benefit of creating more time spent in the booth because not only do they take time to write, but also read what others have written. Then there's the in-booth art project like the Charlotte Convention & Visitors Bureau (CVB) did, allowing attendees to paint on a large blank canvas in the booth. (The CVB provided bright-colored paint, brushes and rollers, and smocks for their "guest artists.") Once the wall was covered with art, they removed a nearly invisible white mask to reveal the Charlotte skyline in vivid color! The final mural was then featured on a follow-up postcard sent after the show.

- **"The Doctor is In"** — Trade show labor and event management company TS Crew drew lots of second looks from attendees at EXHIBITOR*LIVE* when their staff wore white lab coats, stethoscopes, and buttons bearing a witty message to "Cure Exhibit Malpractice." (Which they also handed out to attendees to wear.) In the booth, there was an eyechart-style sign promoting a special offer.

- **"In the Studio" or "On the Air"** — Why not turn your booth into a recording studio? Create a space for attendees to step in front of the camera to share their "ah-ha" moments related to your topic. (Think StoryCorps booths.) Post the videos on your blog and/or social media channels and collect contact information so you can send attendees the link to watch and share their videos. Exhibit Edge did this one year at EXHIBITOR*LIVE* in Las Vegas. You can see my interview in their booth on the ***Trade Show Insights*** blog.

- **Virtual Venue** — Locations like New Orleans or Seattle are easy to recreate in a small space by simply using a backwall graphic with a famous street scene. But I've also seen exhibits that are made to look like the venue they're representing, such as a cruise ship cabin or a hospital room.

- **"Under Construction"** — When you want to market a venue that hasn't been built yet, what's there to showcase beside artist renderings? One CVB used yellow construction tape and hard hats, then featured a 3-D model of their upcoming convention center. Booth visitors were given hard hat keychains imprinted with the CVB name.

You'll find many more clever exhibit themes and designs on my Pinterest boards and on the ***Trade Show Insights*** blog, where you can also watch videos of clever themes and designs showcased at EXHIBITOR*LIVE*. If you're still not sure where to begin to discover a theme, you might want to schedule a brainstorming session, where we spend time on the phone exploring theme ideas and finding the one that really resonates for you and your target audience. This can be one of the most fun parts of the exhibit creation process!

There are many ways to make the most of a small space. Here are a few of the biggest keys to small-booth success (many of which apply to a booth of any size):

- **Tell a story and create an environment** — Stories and emotional connections sell far better than statistics and data. That's why creating a theme is so helpful for making your exhibit more relatable and memorable.

- **Make it inviting and comfortable** — No matter the size of your booth, does it make people want to spend time there and learn more about what you have to offer?

- **Focus on interaction and personal attention** — Create a multisensory experience and use interactive elements such as hands-on demos or various types of technology to get attendees engaged. (We'll cover multisensory elements in more depth in Part 4.)

- **Design with your audience in mind** — Use marketing messages and themes that will draw them in and make them feel like you're reading their mind. (More on this coming up in Part 2.)

The bottom line is that with a small space you've got to maximize every inch without going overboard and appearing cluttered.

Inside the bonus materials for this chapter:

- Photos and/or links to some of the case studies mentioned
- Links to Pinterest boards on exhibit design
- Videos of cool ideas from EXHIBITOR*LIVE*
- My video interview in the Exhibit Edge booth

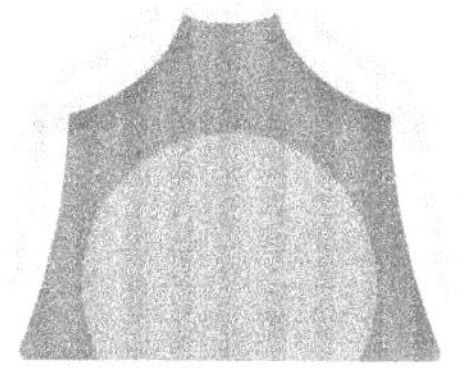

Theme Development: What's Next?

- Decide on the core message you want to communicate.

- Determine what visual theme could best illustrate that message.

- Begin looking for inspiration in a variety of places.

- Brainstorm elements to include in all aspects of your exhibit to support the theme.

Don't design what you like …
design for your audience
and what will best engage
and connect with them.

Part 2:
Consider the Attendees' Perspective

Often when I ask exhibitors how many attendees they want to talk with at a show, I'll hear a number that's well over 50 percent.

Now, unless you're exhibiting at a very small show (say less than 150 attendees), that probably won't ever happen. Talking with that many people just isn't realistic.

I believe those overinflated numbers stem from a fear of "I have to talk with everyone, so I don't risk missing out on talking with the *right* people."

But that's not how it works. Your job is to get inside your ideal prospect's head and communicate to them with every part of your design so that the "right" ones prequalify themselves. You have to meet the expectations they have while also delivering on your brand promise.

Do you know what they want? If not, maybe it's time to do a bit of homework ...

Guess what?
Attendees aren't
coming to the show
just to see you!

They're Just Not That Into You

There's a disorder that nearly every exhibitor suffers from at one point or another. It begins slowly, but can grow to a dangerous level.

It's called "Center of the Universe Syndrome," and it can develop due to event planning stress, lack of education, or just plain laziness. It manifests as either arrogance or indifference, with exhibitors relying too much on outside circumstances (show management, booth location, etc.) to drive traffic to their booth instead of being proactive. Left unchecked, it can reach disastrous proportions and cause complete failure at the show.

So how do you overcome this? Begin by taking steps long before the show to make your booth attractive to attendees, both in appearance and in the activities going on there throughout show hours. Have a reason for attendees to not only enter your space, but to also spend time there learning about your products, services, and the solutions you can provide for them. Make your booth an oasis on the show floor, not a cookie-cutter replica of a dozen other booths.

A lot of exhibitors (as well as some show organizers) still take the "Field of Dreams" approach to trade shows, believing that all they need to do is be there and the attendees will be magically drawn to them. But the fact is that a very small percentage (if any) of the people walking the aisles are there specifically to see what any given booth is offering.

First of all, are you even exhibiting at the right show? Are attendees at that show seeking what you offer, or are you trying to convince them about something they're not even in the market for?

There's no tolerance for one-way conversations anymore — attendees are seeking innovative ideas, fresh perspectives, and a relevant, personalized experience that focuses on their specific needs. You have to delight and inspire by making your message feel as if it is speaking only to a single person, rather than to the masses. Statistics show that 57 percent of customer research takes place before the first contact with a salesperson, so attendees are coming to a show already well-informed. It's no longer about educating people on your product or service, but rather impressing them with how your solution is exactly what they're seeking.

Forget the inward-focused language — whether you're marketing the show or an individual exhibit. Attendees don't ultimately care about your new CEO, your prestigious awards, or the latest patent you've achieved. They simply want to know how you can solve their problems. In order to craft your message, you have to first get inside their heads to understand the psychology of their pain and what solution they're really seeking. Then incorporate that message into all your marketing, before, during and after the show. Use the same language that your prospective clients would use ... no corporate mumbo-jumbo!

When you're working the booth, it also helps to understand body language and buying signals. Learn the right questions to ask and how to tell a story that not only draws them in, but makes them think, "Wow! This company really gets where I'm coming from! They really understand how to help me." Be genuine and friendly, not stuffy or preachy. Let them know that you're truly on their side and ready to be their guide to a solution. (More to come on this in the *YES: Your Exhibit Success* book on marketing and promotions.)

Exhibitors often wish they could read attendees' minds. The report from the Center for Exhibition Industry Research (CEIR), titled "Exhibition Floor Interaction: What Attendees Want," may provide the next best thing. It reveals that attendees' top answers involve product demonstrations and hands-on interaction, which is no great surprise, considering that's one of the greatest benefits of a face-to-face event over online research. Yet too many exhibitors are still lacking in opportunities for attendees to get an immersive experience with their products.

Following closely behind product interaction is the ability to take information with them to review later, whether printed or digital. And the third way attendees want to interact is by engaging with knowledgeable booth staff to learn more about the products, according to the study. But again, exhibitors often fail in this area because the staff is untrained and/or unprepared to answer questions. (More to come on that in the *YES: Your Exhibit Success* book on booth staffing.)

Inside the bonus materials for this chapter:

- Link to access the CEIR report, "Exhibition Floor Interaction: What Attendees Want"

“Mastery of language
affords one remarkable
opportunities.”

Alexandre Dumas

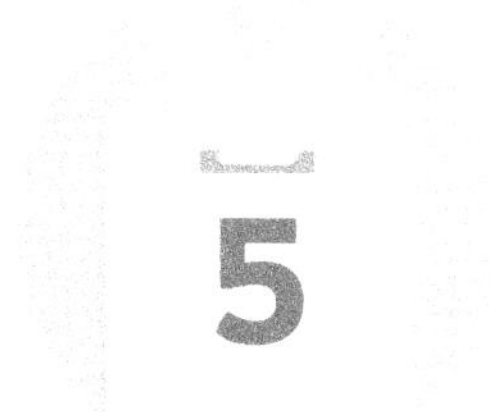

Speaking the Attendees' Language

Do you speak a second language? If so, how did you learn, and how well do you communicate in that language?

Personally, I took one year of French in high school, and although I sounded fairly good at the time, now pretty much all I can do is say hello (*Bonjour!*) and count to 10 ... plus a few other random words.

My husband and I have also had a desire to learn Mandarin for several years, and so we've purchased several books and audio sets. We even attended an introductory workshop and learned some basic pronunciation tips (Mandarin is very tricky, in case you didn't realize). But since we've never really focused on learning the language, about all I know is hello (*Ni hao*) and thank you (*Xiè xiè*). While those are some good basic words to know, they wouldn't get us very far if we were actually in China!

Now you may be thinking that this only relates to international exhibiting, but you would be wrong. Every time you set up a booth, you have to become fluent in the language of the attendees at that show. While that may not involve learning to speak French, Mandarin, Spanish, or any other global language, it still requires focused study.

For example, are your signs and materials in the booth written from the perspective of what your ideal client wants to know? Do you even recognize what that is? You can't use lots of "we" and "us" bullet points and expect attendees to be impressed. No one really cares about how "We've been rated safest in the industry for the past 10 years."

Instead make it all about them and meeting their needs using "you" and "your": "You won't find a safer XYZ product, as ABC Company discovered with their 400% improved safety record." (Then provide a testimonial or case study to back it up.)

Next, lose the corporate-speak! Don't use words such as core competency, integrated solutions, etc. Sometimes I think corporate copywriters need journalists to translate their jargon into plain English. Here's an example of what *not* to do (names removed to protect the guilty):

> *"Our long experience ranges from enterprise brand architecture to complex solution selling. More recently we've concentrated on the changing responsibilities of marketing executives as they face the corporate culture challenges created by the new social media."*

Say what?!! Now I'm pretty sure you don't talk like that, so why would you want to write like that? A good rule of thumb is to share your wording with family or friends outside your industry to see if they can make sense of what you're selling. Or better yet … see if a 10-year-old can figure out what you're talking about. Not that attendees are like 10-year-olds … except they are when it comes to how much effort they want to put into figuring out what you're trying to say!

Inside the bonus materials for this chapter:

- Attendee Language Checklist

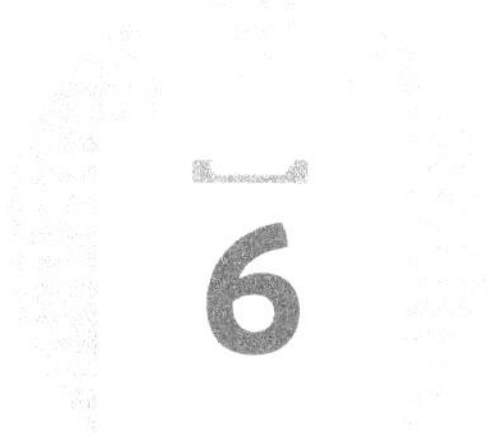

Give Attendees What They Want

When planning your upcoming exhibits, how much do you think about what attendees at that show want ... or are you simply including all the things you (and others who have a say within your company) want to show off?

Perhaps you're not even sure what attendees want in the first place. That's where studies done by the Center for Exhibition Industry Research (CEIR) come in handy. They published a report titled "Quick Guide on Attendee Preferences by Industry Sector" which includes answers from 421 respondents in 14 industries. And while the ranking of answers may vary somewhat by industry, the top two shopping-related reasons attendees go to trade shows are consistent across the board:

1. See new technology
2. Ability to talk to experts

(To see how attendees in your industry ranked, you can purchase the complete report #AC41.15 on the CEIR website.)

Problem is, many exhibitors (and sometimes the shows themselves) fail on one or both counts. While there may be new technology, it's either not featured prominently or not shown off to the best advantage. What if shows created a spotlight area for new tech, or perhaps even had a theater on the show floor where that technology could be presented more in-depth?

Now I know what you're thinking … "What if we have no new technology because we're not a tech company?" Well, I'm sure you have something new to share … and new product introductions comes in as the third reason on that list. The key is to show it off with product demonstrations … or better yet, hands-on interaction with the product. (Both rank high on the list of show floor interaction preferences from the study, by the way.)

Now as for the ability to talk with experts … many exhibitors miss the boat on this one. How many times have you seen a booth filled with only salespeople (or been guilty of this yourself)? It's no secret that they are not necessarily the best option for booth staffers. (In fact, I wrote an entire blog post on this topic.) It's important to have a mix of experts in the booth — technical, customer service, R&D, etc. — who can answer all kinds of questions because getting answers is another primary thing attendees want.

Also don't overlook the non-shopping reasons attendees also cited in the CEIR study, which include getting industry trend insights and improving their job performance. How can you assist attendees with those objectives?

67% of all qualified attendees represent a new prospect and potential customer for exhibiting companies

(Source: CEIR #ACRR1120.12 "Exhibitions Attract New Prospects")

You could offer education, either by offering to lead conference-wide breakout sessions or a session within your own booth. Show how your company is a thought-leader in the industry and on the leading edge of trends. Find out what specific topics your target audience is most hungry for, then address those in your presentations, or in reports you create to give to attendees who provide you with their contact information. Are they looking for a way to compare brands? Create a report on "How to Choose the Right _____ for You" … which of course, gives them all the data they need to see your company as the obvious choice.

Above all, don't ever forget that face-to-face interaction is one of the key advantages of trade shows over other marketing methods. Be sure you take full advantage of that by providing attendees with the 'live' aspects they can't get elsewhere, like hands-on involvement and the ability to meet experts they otherwise might not have access to.

For more in-depth insights on what attendees want, here are a couple more CEIR reports to check out:
- AC32.13 "What Attendees Want from Trade Exhibitions"
- AC40.14 "Exhibition Floor Interaction: What Attendees Want" (Which was discussed more in chapter 4.)

Inside the bonus materials for this chapter:

- Links to access the CEIR reports mentioned
- Link to podcast episode on "The Challenge of Using Salespeople in Your Booth"

Successful brands – or
exhibits – don't stand
out by blending in.

Branding Your Exhibit

How well does your exhibit reflect your company's brand?

If you answered anything less than "totally," then you have work to do.

Now we're not talking about simply including your logo. In fact, would your display even work if your logo was removed, or would it be indistinguishable from your competitors?

As stated before, a trade show exhibit does not exist separately from the rest of your marketing. Instead, it should be a three-dimensional version of all your other marketing methods.

For example, if you emphasize innovation and fun in your advertising, make your exhibit reflect that. Use whimsical colors and graphics. Dress your staff in clever, color-coordinated attire (perhaps a fun print vest or tie). Create multisensory experiences that also communicate your out-of-the-box corporate brand.

But if your existing corporate brand is more focused on traits such as reliability or exclusivity, your exhibit needs to be more serious. Use more elegant or "serious" colors and dress your staff in more traditional conservative apparel. Use multisensory experiences that create a sense of trust and confidence.

Areas to Consider (we'll delve into most of these in later chapters):

- Colors & graphics
- Booth architecture
- Staff attire
- Mood music or other sounds
- Product displays
- Aromas

Remember: An exhibit that works for a company like Nickelodeon or Kia Motors won't work for the History Channel or Lexus. Likewise, you need to decide what "personality" your exhibit needs to reflect.

Create a Brand Manual

There's one simple tool that can make your exhibit design easier, whether you're a small business doing only a couple of shows each year, or an exhibit manager in charge of multiple exhibits at dozens of shows worldwide.

Having a brand manual and style guide will help to maintain a consistent look and feel for exhibits of all sizes and for all divisions within a company. Some of the topics to address in the manual include: how the company name and tagline will appear, what colors can be used and how, what flooring and lighting to use, how products are to be displayed, and more. By having the big issues well-defined, it means your look and message is consistent while still allowing for some degree of creativity at each show.

Stand Out, Don't Blend In

Think about the general look of exhibits at any given industry show and how they all tend to look the same. Often even the color choices and signage tends to blend from one booth to another. What can you do to be different or give the show floor more personality?

And don't use the excuse that you're exhibiting someplace "serious" like a medical or tech-industry show. I've seen exhibitors there who have done some really memorable things that stood out. (You'll discover some of those examples in later chapters.)

The benefits of getting creative don't stop at just getting attention at the show — it also makes your booth more memorable in the days and weeks that follow so the attendees are more likely to think of you when they're ready to buy.

Inside the bonus materials for this chapter:

- Link to podcast interview with Ben Baker on branding
- Brand Manual & Style Guide checklist

"The greatest risk to man
is not that he aims too
high and misses, but that
he aims too low and hits."

Michaelangelo

Attendee Perspective: What's Next?

- Research what attendees in your audience want and what their concerns are.

- Focus on creating a two-way conversation with your message or theme.

- Clean up the inward-focused corporate speak.

- Convey your brand and message accurately and consistently.

- Develop elements that attendees can only experience while face-to-face in your exhibit.

You should keep up with trends,
but use them to develop
your own style — It's all
in the interpretation!

Part 3:
Look for Design Inspiration

If you're waiting for inspiration to strike, good luck! Instead, you need to be proactive and find ways to help it along. Stop saying you're not creative — get up from your desk and go for a "walkabout" as the Aussies say (out in the fresh air if possible) and take photos of things that catch your eye for whatever reason.

Study trends to see what's new with shapes, colors, materials and more. Find examples you like and note why they appeal to you. Create an online portfolio (Pinterest works well for this) and share that with your exhibit designer.

"You can't depend on your eyes
when your imagination
is out of focus."

Mark Twain

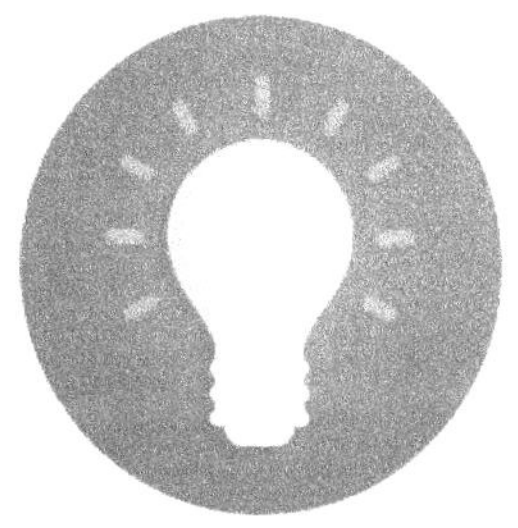

7 Sources of Design Inspiration

At the EXHIBITOR Show in Las Vegas one year, I coordinated a field trip called "TSI: Trade Show Investigation." I led two teams of exhibitors (investigators) along the Strip, stopping at New York New York, the Venetian, and other locations to "gather evidence" of ideas they could use in their future exhibit displays. The idea was to cause participants to stop and examine the elements around them to discover what makes a place engaging and memorable.

Want to do your own TSI Field Trip? Here's where to look:

- **Retail stores** — Because an exhibit booth is essentially a temporary store, it's no surprise that many of the designers of exhibit displays also design for retail. So why is it that so few exhibitors study how retailers use their store windows, signage, and merchandise displays to attract attention and create a desire to purchase? Walk the sidewalks of virtually any shopping district and study the windows that grab your attention. Is it because of the colors or props used? Perhaps there's an element of surprise or whimsy? Or maybe it's the big, bold signage that catches your eye. Make notes and analyze why it works. (We'll cover more ideas from retail in the next chapter.)

- **Museums/Galleries** — If retail stores are one parent of trade show exhibits, museums are likely the other, and they often share the same design houses. But while retail displays are typically static, museums are created with a focus on interactivity, engaging the visitor in a story. Color plays a role here too, along with lighting, traffic flow, technology, and often multisensory elements. How can your booth tell a story and invite exploration? What opportunities can you give attendees to interact while tapping into their emotions?

- **Hotels & Restaurants** — For those who exhibit often in major cities, spending time in hotels and restaurants comes with the territory. But how frequently do you use that as an opportunity for research? The truth is that today's hospitality climate is highly competitive and even hotels that aren't high-end are taking steps to brand themselves and create welcoming environments. If you've ever been to Vegas, you know that hotels there pull out all the stops to impress guests and create loyalty. From the moment you walk in the door, you feel you've been transported to another continent or time period (or both). In addition to the atmosphere and multisensory elements, hotels and restaurants also have multiple activity zones. In hotels, there's the lobby and front desk (welcome area), the business center (work area), ballrooms (entertainment area), and of course the restaurant, which also has its own zones for entry, eat-in, take-out, and more. How can you incorporate these ideas in your booth?

- **Airports** — Don't laugh! These days, airports, like hotels, are scrambling to become more enjoyable and memorable. The Charlotte Douglas International Airport is famous for a long row of white rocking chairs with a grand piano nearby. Some fliers actually hope for a long enough layover that they can snag a few minutes rocking their cares away. Baltimore's

Thurgood Marshall Airport caters to road-weary families with an aviation-themed play area. What unexpected elements can you offer in your booth to cater to attendees' less obvious needs?

- **Expos Outside Your Industry** — While some shows may be off-limits if you're not an industry insider, others are more open to visitors, plus there are consumer shows held in most every city throughout the year. Walk the show floor to see what catches your eye, and why. Which booths are the most popular? What are some of the most innovative and engaging elements?

- **Theater** — Anyone who's worked an expo would agree that Shakespeare's famous quote, "All the world's a stage" could easily be tweaked to "All the trade show's a stage." So it's no great stretch to see how the thespian world holds inspiration for exhibits in set design, lighting, and signage. (Is it any wonder people collect those classic theater posters?)

- **Stadiums & Arenas** — While this one may not be as obvious, there are lessons to learn from these venues. Today's state-of-the-art stadiums are designed with high-tech tools for enhanced fan engagement and laid out to create efficient traffic flow. They also inspire a social experience where fans interact with each other. How can your booth be more accommodating and engaging for attendees?

No matter where you turn, there are tons of inspirational places just waiting for you to explore. Be open to inspiration when you least expect it and don't try to force ideas; just let them simmer and see what emerges.

Inside the bonus materials for this chapter:

- Links to Pinterest boards on exhibit design
- TSI Field Trip observation worksheet (with tips on how to record observations)

Your design plan should be created based on the goals you have for your exhibit. If your goal is sales, you'll want space for in-depth sales conversations and hands-on demonstrations, while a goal of awareness or lead generation will mean you're more focused on branding messages that are fun and memorable.

Trade Show Booth = Retail Store

Have you ever thought of your trade show booth as a retail store? You should!

During a trade show, your booth is your storefront. You need to design it in order to create a positive experience for the show's visitors. So think like retail owners, whether you are one or not. When you sketch your basic booth layout, make sure it includes:

- Good traffic flow (open, inviting design with easy entrance and exit; no barriers!)
- Merchandising/product displays (clearly identified; include features & benefits)
- Adequate work areas (for presentations, demonstrations, lead collection, and also storage space to keep the booth clutter-free)
- Signage (appealing and informational with clear and definitive corporate identity)
- Lighting (creative and appropriate)

Plan to involve multiple senses in your booth. People process information using a combination of the senses, according to Harold D. Stolovitch and Erica J. Keeps in chapter 3 of *Telling Ain't Training*. Here's how much information is processed by each:

- 83% sight
- 11% hearing
- 3.5% smell
- 1.5% touch
- 1% taste

But don't let those numbers mislead you. Part of the reason that sight is ranked so high is because we can see much farther than we can touch or taste. And keep in mind that those percentages increase exponentially when multiple senses are stimulated.

There just might be some truth to the saying, "in one ear and out the other." According to a study conducted by researchers at the University of Iowa, people don't remember things they hear nearly as well as those they see or touch.* (Just think back to how much you remember from all those lectures you heard in school, versus the hands-on science experiments or art projects you participated in.)

The more senses you combine, the higher the retention rate. In addition, you are creating an overall experience for your visitors, much like the theme restaurant, Rainforest Cafe. Restaurant guests start by seeing trees and various jungle critters, hearing the sound of a waterfall and occasional "thunderstorms," touching all kinds of merchandise in the gift shop, smelling not only the food but also the mist from the waterfall, and of course tasting the food. If you've ever been to a Rainforest Cafe, just reading this description probably transported you back to your experience there. Isn't that what you want visitors at your booth to take away with them?

We'll delve into multisensory elements in much more depth in Part 4.

Citation: Bigelow J, Poremba A (2014) Achilles' Ear? Inferior Human Short-Term and Recognition Memory in the Auditory Modality. PLoS ONE 9(2): e89914. https://doi.org/10.1371/journal.pone.0089914

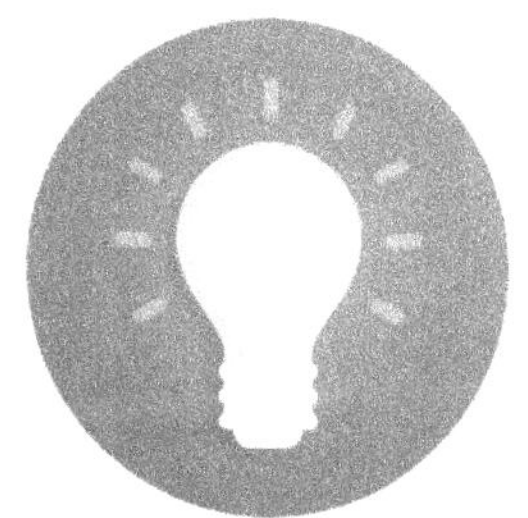

Design Inspiration: What's Next?

- Create your own TSI Field Trip to look for inspiration in unexpected places.

- Study retail store displays, signage and more to discover what works and why … not only to catch attention, but also to generate sales.

- Review Pinterest, Behance and other design websites to see what's current and fresh, then create your online inspiration board.

**Experiential = Memorable!
Create positive emotions.**

Part 4:
Create a Multisensory Experience

We don't live in a one-dimensional world. We don't even stop at 3-D — we live in a multisensory world, filled with sights, sounds, smells, tastes and textures.

So why then do so many exhibitors (and exhibit designers) focus almost exclusively on looks?

It's a fact that the brands which create the strongest emotional bonds with their audience use multisensory marketing to achieve it. Great design goes beyond a look to create a story, which in turn creates a memorable experience.

Create a mood or atmosphere
in your booth using a theme and
multisensory components —
make attendees *feel* something!

Creating an Experience

Exhibitors should strive to create a memorable experience for attendees, but at one show that was taken to a new level.

While it wasn't very attractive from the outside, a giant box in one exhibitor's booth served as a magnet for attendees. In fact, there was often a line waiting to get a look inside.

The tour began with a brief video presentation explaining how several companies had come together to create a suite of software to streamline work in that industry. All relevant data and applications were stored on a central computer, yet could be used in real-time collaboration via Webcams and shared information.

Next, guests were led on a walk-through tour demonstrating the process at work. First, actors dressed as field workers set up the problem and Web-conferenced with experts (more actors) back in the office, analyzing trends and identifying potential problems.

Next, guests observed the experts at work in the company offices, studying the data that had been sent in from the field and searching for inconsistencies. Then guests watched another team of experts using simulations to analyze data and play out "what if" scenarios. The final stop on the tour was a company executive on an airplane, who was viewing the data on her laptop before giving the final go-ahead for changes necessary to solve the current problem.

Following the tour, each guest's badge was scanned and everyone received a hard-shell CD case containing two CD-ROM samplers of the company's software. (This was obviously a while back … there would be other delivery methods available today, but the point is it was a gift that felt very substantial and worth the time spent.)

So what did this company do differently? First of all, they made their booth more like a trip to an amusement park than a sales pitch. Instead of selling their software, they allowed attendees to eavesdrop on the real-world applications and watch the process unfold. Next, there were no hit-and-run attendees. Everyone had to have their badge scanned before they could exit the giant box. And finally, the giveaway tied in beautifully with the message — everyone went home with a demo so they could learn more about the software.

You can use this "magical mystery" concept to create exclusivity and intrigue, creating more desire for attendees to get inside. While exhibits designed in this way break the rule of being open and inviting, they make up for it by creating the "velvet rope" effect of a high-end club because the attendee's badge must be swiped in order to enter.

But keep in mind that what awaits them inside must live up to the anticipation or else word will quickly spread that it's not worth attendees' time. Also consider that even though you may generate far more leads using this technique, they're not all necessarily going to be hot leads. So be sure to have a great lead nurturing plan in place to capitalize on their memories of the booth. Maintain your theme, branding, and message when following up, and include links for them to learn more about what they saw in the booth. (More to come on that in the *YES: Your Exhibit Success* book on marketing and promotions.)

11

What a Theme Park Can Teach Exhibitors

No, we're not talking about turning your exhibit into a theme park … at least not literally. But there's no doubt that when it comes to memorable experiences, theme parks are king. Everything and everyone at the park is focused on the guest's experience and how to exceed expectations. So is it magic, or how do they do it?

Here are some of their strategies:

- **Pay attention to details.** At a theme park, no small detail is ignored. From staff uniforms to landscaping, everything is in alignment and there's no disconnect. If a piece of trash finds its way onto the path, there's an employee nearby to whisk it away so the illusion won't be spoiled. Likewise in your exhibit, be sure that you're presenting the right image and that it's consistent. If your booth looks fantastic, but your staff is sloppy or lazy, that ruins the overall impression.

- **Tell a carefully designed story.** These parks take advantage of theming and multisensory cues to make the story come to life. Color, aroma, taste, music and touch are all elements in crafting a realistic atmosphere. Even waiting in line for the rides becomes an immersion in the story, painting a picture of what's to come. To create a truly memorable exhibit, you must first get clear on what story or message you want to convey. Once you have that, begin to think through how you'll illustrate it with props, color, and experiential elements. Give visitors that feeling of "Wow!" when they're in your booth.

- **Always look through the eyes of the visitor,** considering their feelings, frustrations and path of travel. Park employees are taught to tune into the needs of those who want help, before they even ask for it and to create personalized experiences whenever possible by not sticking to a script. The best way to accomplish this at a trade show is to listen to the visitor and pay attention to what they tell you. Don't greet everyone the same way or expect them to all respond the same. Role-play before the show to better anticipate questions and formulate effective answers. Design your booth in a way that leads visitors down the path — literally by having good traffic flow and signage, as well as figuratively by guiding their interaction with your company and products.

- **Never confuse onstage with backstage.** At some parks, employees even have secret passages to get from one part of the park to another so they're never out of place. When you're at a trade show, you're always onstage! Be careful what you say and do, both inside and outside the booth, because someone's always watching and listening.

- **One key to a happy audience is a happy, well-trained staff.** It makes a world of difference in a visitor's experience when it's obvious that the staff enjoys being there and truly cares about them. New employees are not allowed to work in the park until they've been properly and thoroughly trained. Why don't exhibitors care that much about having a staff that can make a world of difference for attendee experiences? (More to come on this in the *YES: Your Exhibit Success* book on booth staffing.)

So do you need to have an over-the-top, in-your-face theme with lots of flash and sizzle? Of course not! There are lots of easy and effective ways to create atmosphere and connect with attendees, as you'll discover in upcoming chapters.

Sensory branding is tied to
memory, emotions and feelings.

12

Multisensory Marketing

Want to increase the chances an attendee will remember their specific experience in your booth? Stimulate more of their senses!

Think about it ... how do you shop in a store? Most people sniff and squeeze produce at the grocery store, touch fabrics in a clothing store, or sit on chairs in a furniture store. The same idea applies in a trade show booth: give them ways to interact and experience your brand.

Sadly, most marketing is designed to only appeal to one sense (sight), but to fully reinforce your message aim to include stimuli for at least three of the senses. Just be sure all those sensory messages are consistent — don't send conflicting signals.

In chapter 5 of my book, ***Build a Better Trade Show Image***, I shared the story of the Superior Communications booth. It's still one of my favorite examples of how to incorporate all the senses into your exhibit (think 5-D).

In order to create a relaxed atmosphere in the middle of a very high-tech cellular industry show, Superior Communications came up with the concept, "When you work with us, it's like R&R." They decided to use two pop-up campers for conference rooms. From there, they built the theme, "Camp Superior," creating redwood trees, a rock fountain (named "Lake Superior"), rustic trail signs, and even an artificial campfire. They continued setting the mood with sounds of crickets and frogs, and the occasional coyote howl. Products were displayed on a clothesline hung between the trees, along with custom-designed Superior boxer shorts. (You'll find photos of the booth on the **Trade Show Insights** blog.)

So let's break down the techniques Superior used and how you can create a similar multisensory experience.

Sight

While sight is the most common sense relied on for first impressions, it can create lasting ones as well.

Color is one of the most popular tools for creating sensory cues for sight, and up to 85 percent of people say that color plays a primary role in the decision to purchase a product. But there are many other tools that come into play here as well, including graphics, motion, lighting, and more. We'll cover many of these in more depth in later chapters.

Sound

The right sound can impact attendees' perception of your company or products and can also be used to boost recall after the show.

You could use what's known as soundscaping to create a mood (like Superior did with the nature noises). Music is another obvious tool, as you've likely noticed in retail stores. But what you may not realize is that the style and tempo can influence behavior — restaurants have discovered that fast songs help with turnover, while slow ones increase spending. However there are two important details to note if you do plan on using music in your booth: watch your sound levels and be sure you have proper music licensing.

The sound of your actual product can also be used to your advantage. For example, did you know that cereal manufacturers engineer the crunch sound their product makes? And did you realize that smart phone cameras were designed to emulate the sound of an actual camera shutter?

Finally, don't forget about the power of a jingle or sound trademark, such as the familiar three notes of the NBC TV Network or Intel's five notes.

Touch

As mentioned earlier, people shop based on the feel of a product. Various fabrics and textures send different messages: silk conveys elegance and drama, while denim or burlap are more casual and relaxed. Even the feel of the paper you print your materials on can send a message about your company and products, increasing attendee confidence and desire to buy from you.

Besides texture, there are many other factors involved in the perception of touch: temperature, weight, shape and more. One of the best ways to utilize this sense is by letting attendees handle your products so they get a feel for them.

Smell

It's a mind-boggling fact that the human nose can identify and recall as many as 10,000 distinct scents (far more than tastes). It's also been proven that because our sense of smell has a direct link to our brain, aromas can influence mood, concentration and emotions.

Ever consider how you react when you smell chocolate chip cookies? Freshly-cut grass? Or what about cinnamon or pine trees?

Scientists have discovered that various scents can be used to induce calm, excitement or nostalgia. Here are a few nearly-universal scent messages that might be beneficial in your booth:

      Adventure = Pine woods or spice

      Traditional = Leather, cedar

> Comfort/relaxing = Vanilla, cotton, ocean breeze
>
> Sophisticated = Musk
>
> Childhood/nostalgia = Bubble gum, crayons, chocolate chip cookies, apple pie
>
> Happy = Citrus
>
> Energized & alert = Peppermint or spice

You could follow the lead of some well-known hotels, retailers, and even banks to create your own custom-blended signature scent to inspire a one-of-a-kind experience. (Did you know the scent of Crayola crayons is trademarked?)

Your chosen scent can be broadcast far and wide using scent machines (although as with sound, be careful of how much extends outside your booth), or carefully controlled to create an immersive experience with scents emitted on cue as attendees watch a presentation. Use it to enhance your exhibit theme and personality. For example, I remember one display where the look was colorful, oversized flowers and butterflies reminiscent of children's picture books, which were paired with scents of bubble gum and chocolate chip cookies as you entered.

Remember back to scratch-and-sniff books when you were a kid? That same technology can now be incorporated into print materials using scented inks and papers.

Keep in mind that incorporating scent marketing requires a responsibility to use it ethically and with consideration to those who suffer from allergies and other sensitivities. You'll also want to choose scents that appeal to your demographic. There's more to come on scent marketing in the following chapter.

Taste

This one is closely tied to the sense of smell, but is often the most difficult to incorporate unless you're displaying food products in your booth. However, innovative exhibitors manage to weave taste into their product's story in a creative way.

Often you'll see coffee bars or ice cream stations in a booth. But at one EXHIBITOR Show, designer Steelhead Productions decided to create a gourmet Lemonade Lounge in citrus colors with a Vegas vibe. Now keep in mind, this was 2009, at the height of the time when the economy was leaving a bad taste in everyone's mouth. So with a theme of "Turning sour budgets into sweet exhibits," Steelhead served up glasses of lemonade in a bright and cheery oasis while booth visitors were entertained by a flair bartender. Drinking glasses on a shelf behind the bar served as a portfolio with photos of previous client projects inside. There were cardboard coasters branded with "Lemonade Lounge" and the company website, along with a "reverse tip jar" which held small cards printed with tips for attendees.

One caution when planning to serve any kind of food in your booth: you'll need to make sure you're properly licensed and have cleared it with show management. At some venues, you can only use their approved caterer, which may come at a considerable expense.

A creative way to tie in the sense of taste without actually serving food is to use taste wording or analogies: "Ingredients list," "Taste of ___" or "Cooking up ideas for ____."

Inside the bonus materials for this chapter:

- Photos and/or links to some of the case studies mentioned
- Audio interview with Simon Harrop on "Incorporating Multisensory Marketing"
- Multisensory checklist
- More information on music licensing

Scent can trigger powerful
memories – of a food, a place,
or a person – which transport
you across space and time.

Scent of a Trade Show

Never ignore the importance of scent.

One year at the EXHIBITOR Show, I attended a session on using scent in exhibits taught by a university professor. She shared some of the science behind using fragrances to impact audiences, as well as how to choose the right fragrance for a brand based on examples from both retail and hospitality markets. (In fact, many hotels have developed custom blends known as "scent logos.") And if you think that using fragrance in your booth must be expensive, think again. There are options in all price ranges, from scented ink or papers to scent strips to scent disbursement machines.

Later while leading the "TSI: Trade Show Investigation" field trip at that same event, I was keenly aware of the scents (or lack of) at each location we visited. Some nearly made my eyes water because they were so strong (gardenias, anyone?) and others were mere hints of citrus or florals.

But perhaps the most important illustration in the use of fragrance came on my flight home later that week. I was quietly sitting in my usual window seat, when a retired couple sat in my row. The lady took the middle seat, and immediately I knew I was in trouble. She was wearing one of those "grandma-floral" colognes, and way too much of it. As she buckled in, I reached for the overhead vent and pointed it right in front of my face to diffuse as much scent as possible. I did manage to survive the two-and-a-half hour flight without getting a massive headache, but was I ever ready to get off that plane!

The lesson here? No matter how good you think a fragrance smells, not everyone will like it, and some may even have strong negative reactions. So as the professor shared in her workshop, make sure that whatever method you use to distribute a scent in your booth can be stopped at any moment. Too much of a good thing could leave your customers a bit woozy and sorry that they ever stopped in your booth. And that's certainly not the message you want to be sending!

The Smell of Success

Can you smell that? Mmmmmmm ... smells like fresh-baked chocolate chip cookies. Does that make you feel warm and comfortable? Want to relax and stay awhile?

Now move on to the next scent ... fresh-squeezed orange juice. Did your mood just change from cozy to awake and energized?

Scientists have studied the effects of scent for years. In the past decade, aromatherapy has become mainstream as a way to use fragrances to evoke or change mood. So why not use that technique in your next trade show exhibit?

Retailers who use scent technologies to create a mood find that visits last longer and sales increase significantly, even if the scent has nothing to do with the product being sold. (Which could explain why even banks are beginning to use scent marketing technologies.)

And if you're still not convinced that using familiar scents can make a difference to your audience, consider the story of a Florida hospital. Wanting to make the experience of having an MRI scan more pleasant, they decorated the rooms with ocean murals and used an aroma machine with coconut and lavender fragrances. Their patients are now much more relaxed!

Scent Strategy

How can you incorporate scent in your exhibit? If your focus is in any way food-related, that's pretty obvious. But what about using a fresh-cut grass aroma to enhance an outdoors theme, or a salty sea breeze scent to reinforce a beach theme?

But don't just spray fragrance all over your display. Use it strategically to reach out and draw attendees in (often food scents work best for this) or to reinforce your theme, like the examples above. If your exhibit has a not-so-pleasant smell (say the machine you're demonstrating puts off a strong industrial odor), you can use a more inviting scent to tone it down and make attendees more likely to stick around.

By using this often-overlooked sense, you can not only help attendees relax and spend more time in your booth, but also forge a stronger emotional bond and create more positive memories of your company.

Inside the bonus materials for this chapter:

- Links to resources for scent marketing

Rise above the confusion!
If you create a unique experience,
people are certain to
remember your booth.

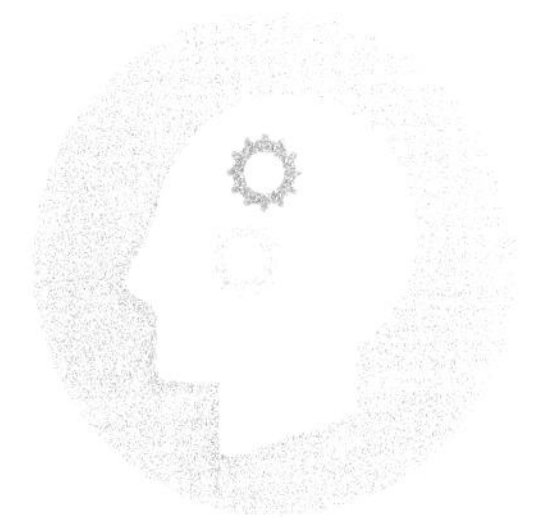

Multisensory Experience: What's Next?

- Determine what feeling or message you want to convey to attendees (and what sensory cues they might relate to best).

- Brainstorm how you can incorporate at least three of the five senses in your booth.

- What elements can you use to create a "WOW" Factor that creates an experience to remember?

Is it clear at first glance who
you are and what you do?

Part 5:
Design with the End in Mind

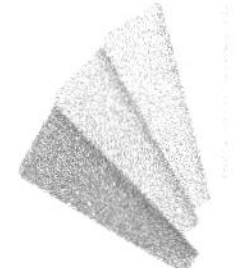

Think back … the last time you designed a new exhibit booth, how much time did you take to plan before jumping into the design process? Did you answer a series of questions in-house before getting bids and renderings from a designer?

Too often, exhibitors rush into exhibit design, with the only criteria being "we want a whole new look" (and oh, yes … easy on the budget). Often very little time is spent considering things like colors, moods, and essential design details. This leaves the field wide open for the designer, and they may let their creativity run wild. However, when the sketches come back, it may not be at all what the client (you) wanted.

Like so many business challenges, it all comes down to communication. Talk it over as a team and know what your basic criteria includes. Then go to your exhibit designer with a detailed plan. You'll make their job so much easier, plus you'll be much happier with the end result. When I sit down with my exhibitor clients, we go through an in-depth list of design planning questions to determine their message, booth layout, design elements, and more — all before they ever even meet with an exhibit designer.

Although you may be tempted to skip parts of the upcoming chapters because they seem too meticulous for you … don't do it. I promise you'll benefit whether you're an exhibit manager who outsources everything to your designer or an entrepreneur who wears multiple hats in the development of your booth. By understanding the tools and how they work, it provides a basis for your decision-making process and strategic choices that will best meet your needs and solve your exhibit design challenges.

Be aware of design trends, but don't blindly copy them.

Exhibit Display Types Defined

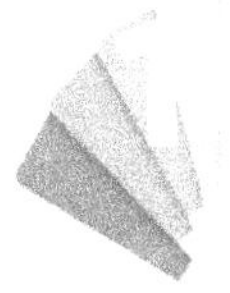

If you're new to the world of exhibiting (or perhaps even if you've been around awhile), you're likely a bit confused by all the terminology, especially when it comes to the types of displays. So here are some basic definitions for you.

Table Top Displays

This small portable display fits on top of a six- or eight-foot table and is often the starting point for new exhibitors, especially those on a tight budget. It's also a smart idea for a smaller show, like a local Chamber of Commerce expo. But just because it's small doesn't mean it can't be creative and fun! Table tops have come a long way from what you may remember at school science fairs. Many of them now feature attractive curved elements, fabric graphics, lights, and even shelving — just like their larger counterparts.

Portable or Pop-up Displays

The term "portable" refers to a display that's lightweight, easily transported, and usually can be set up in just a few minutes. Over the past three decades these displays, which often have collapsible tube structures, have become a convenient and cost-effective alternative for exhibits — so much so that it's often the most common design on the show floor. Setup is quick and simple (the frames on some designs virtually "pop up" into place). Depending on the type of frame, fabric or graphic panels are typically attached using magnets, snap rings, or a strip of plastic beading along the edge (silicone-edge graphics, or SEG). The caution with this style is that your graphics must be unique and very eye-catching so that your exhibit doesn't look like all the other portables on the show floor.

Modular or Hybrid Displays

These displays feature interchangeable elements or panels that can be reconfigured in a variety of ways, allowing an exhibitor to create a unique identity with both the structure and message. This is perfect for companies who exhibit at many different shows and require different booth sizes or branding at each one. While the original modular displays were often made up of laminate panels and frames, today's hybrids combine engineered aluminum frames, tension fabric, and elegant laminate panels with wood, glass, shelving, tablet kiosks … you name it. There's basically no limit to the design options now available to exhibitors in every budget.

Custom Displays

Companies that do large inline or island displays with equally large budgets often opt for a custom design. Need to incorporate massive pieces of equipment or have a demo kitchen in your booth? No problem! A custom exhibit can accommodate all your specific requirements. But since these designs are often built with large metal structures and hardwall panels, they require hiring show labor for setup. That said, there's nothing like a custom exhibit to create a truly signature look and memorable impression on the show floor … if your budget and marketing goals align.

Inside the bonus materials for this chapter:

- Link to see photos of exhibit display types

View from the Aisle

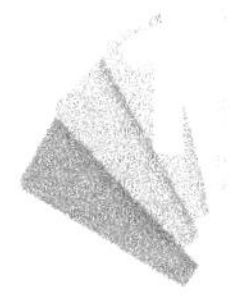

When was the last time you looked at your exhibit from a visitor's perspective?

Have you stepped into the aisle and looked at what's the most prominent thing that catches your eye? Is it what you want to be featuring? If you've been having trouble getting the attention of prospects, you may discover that your booth is not speaking their language.

Does your staff look and act friendly? If not, they may be driving people away. Do an attitude check.

Is it clear who you are and what you do? Sometimes exhibitors are so focused on their tagline that they forget to feature their company name. So you provide "The Fastest Service in the West," but who are you?

Once you learn to look at the exhibiting process from the other side of the aisle, you'll start having better results inside the booth.

And speaking of the aisles …

Trade Show Commandment #2:
You shall not create barriers to traffic.

So many times at shows, first glance down the aisles gives the illusion that the show is overcrowded with attendees. But as you walk the floor, you discover that the reason the aisles are full is because no one can get into any of the booths!

The most common barrier used is the infamous six-foot table. For some reason, everyone thinks the only place it fits is along the aisle. Not so! Rethink your booth floor plan. As the saying goes, "move it or lose it."

While walking one particular show, I noticed the aisles were almost completely clogged. It turns out that wasn't due to a massive quantity of attendees, but rather because virtually every exhibitor was either sitting or standing behind tables along the aisle. This created a barrier and wasted valuable booth space. Sadly, this isn't rare behavior, especially in 10-by-10-foot exhibits. But it can be easily corrected.

First of all, instead of placing the table along the aisle, run it along one side of the booth and stand beside it. This works especially well for

---

The 10 Commandments of Booth Staffing

1. You shall not sit.
2. You shall not create barriers to traffic.
3. You shall not eat or drink.
4. You shall not accost people in the aisles.
5. You shall not talk to your co-workers (or on cell phones).
6. You shall not fill your booth with staffers.
7. You shall not put your hands in your pockets.
8. You shall not put out every piece of literature or giveaway you have.
9. You shall not leave early (or arrive late).
10. You shall smile!

Reprinted from Build a Better Trade Show Image *©2002 by Marlys K. Arnold*

---

sampling items, since attendees must actually enter your booth to try your product. For even more impact, be sure to add some type of interaction or motion that draws people in.

Next, instead of piling stacks of literature on the table, use waterfall racks. These add vertical elements and are less cluttered. Another way to create height in your display is with a stair-step platform on the table to display products. You'll be amazed how much better you can showcase multiple items this way rather than on a flat tabletop.

If you feel you absolutely must have something along the aisle, use only a small podium and leave plenty of room for people to walk out of the aisle and get them into *your space.*

Design for Flow

Your booth space should be designed to suit your needs and facilitate your goals — will you want space for lead gathering, product demonstrations, meeting areas, storage, etc.? Consider how you want traffic to flow through your space and design accordingly.

If you're doing a product launch, put that in the spotlight. Have a theater area for the unveiling, surrounded by hands-on product demonstration areas. I saw this done very creatively at a construction industry show once. The manufacturer had a huge island space that was largely walled off — breaking Commandment #2, but in a good way.

At the entrance to the space, there was a movie theater-style rope-and-stanchion area where attendees lined up to get in at specific times. Once inside the large theater space, they sat through a short presentation that concluded with the curtain opening to reveal the company's latest piece of large construction equipment. Attendees were then allowed to walk around the machine to get a closer look. And as they exited the back of the theater, there were video simulators where they could "sit and drive," getting a feel for how the machine functioned.

Design for Safety & Accessibility

Eliminating barriers isn't only important to increase traffic flow in your booth. Sometimes those barriers can be a safety hazard as well.

Too few exhibitors or exhibit designers take into consideration the disabilities some attendees face. Raised floors may be impressive, but are they safe for attendees with physical disabilities? What about two-story booth layouts — is there a way for those who can't climb stairs to have the same experience on the first floor?

This issue became painfully obvious to me as I walked one particular show with a friend in a scooter and saw how many exhibits she couldn't enter. So I did a *Trade Show Insights* podcast interview with Joan Eisenstodt and Lee Jacobia to get their first-hand perspective on what exhibitors can do to make their booths more accessible and welcoming to all.

On another podcast episode, interpreter Susan Layton shares advice on how to communicate with deaf attendees.

Inside the bonus materials for this chapter:

- Links to podcast interviews on accessibility and communicating with deaf attendees

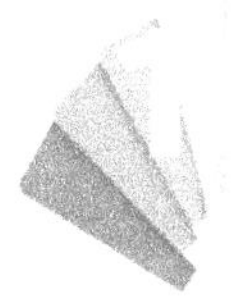

Don't Make Me Squint!

You've been there … you're driving past a billboard on the highway, but it has tiny little type (or way too much), so you squint to read it as you zip past at 65 MPH. Ultimately, you have no idea what it said.

Major fail on the part of that advertiser (and their designer).

But it's not so different on the trade show floor. At show after show, I see displays that weren't designed to be readable, or at least that's the end result. So here are some essential tips for designing graphics and signage that stands out and gets noticed — in a good way!

- **Fonts and font sizes matter.** Go for readable over quirky. Trust me … I'm a true fontaholic (800+ and counting installed on my computer), but only a few of them are appropriate for exhibit signage. Sure you want to avoid using generic fonts (Arial, Helvetica, Times — you know, the ones that came installed on your computer), but there are plenty more basic fonts out there to choose from these days. As a general rule, you want bolder fonts vs. thinner ones, but you can sometimes mix different weights of the same font to create emphasis. In fact, that's another key point: don't mix a bunch of different fonts. Pick a couple that contrast well with each other. (Many fonts now come in "families" that allow for mixing and matching styles all within one font.) When it

Good Signage Fonts	**Not for Signage**
Good serif	Hard-to-read serif
Good sans serif	**Bad sans serif**
Gives illusion of script	*Hard-to-read script*
Properly spaced	**Too tight**
Good handwriting	Too-thin handwriting
Good & bold	Too thin

comes to large text, sans serif (those fonts without the little 'feet' on each letter) tend to work best for readability. (Which is also a good reason to avoid using italics.) Use a simple, bold font that is easily readable from at least 10-20 feet away (depending on the size of your booth). While some creative fonts can be cute and clever for print materials, they may not be clear from that distance, and extremely thin fonts will never work. Go for thicker fonts and be sure the contrast between font color and background lends itself to legibility as well, which leads us to ...

- **Contrast is key.** Even if you've chosen a great font, it won't be readable if you put gray letters on a light blue background. You want a font color that's in high contrast to the background. For example, yellow text will pop off a black or navy background, but will be very difficult to read on lime green or light gray. There's a reason why road signs are typically black letters on white backgrounds or white letters on a dark green or blue background! Monochromatic colors or those in the same scale of light/dark take much closer examination to read, and you don't have that luxury as people are cruising by your booth. Also, stay away from combining opposite colors (like green on red or blue on orange) because they tend to have a vibrating effect. We'll expand on this concept in chapter 18. (And you'll find some actual examples of good and bad color combinations in the bonus materials.)

- **Give words room to breathe.** Don't crowd letters or lines of text too close together. Also be sure you're not piling text on top of a busy background that competes or obscures your message.

- **Simplicity = Maximum impact.** Keep your words to a minimum and avoid using technobabble. Again, think about those classic green highway signs: they don't try to fit three paragraphs onto one sign — they use minimal words to convey the most important information, making it simple to grasp the message as you pass by. Stick with no more than seven words in your headline. If you do need to communicate multiple points, use a bullet list to make it easier to comprehend. (This also goes back to giving the words room to breathe.)

Even directional signage is more likely
to be read when colors and visuals
are included in the right way.
Use less text and more compelling
visuals to create a focal point.

Dynamic = bold, action shot
Static = boring product shot

- **Keep primary text at or above eye level.** Too many exhibit graphics run text nearly all the way to the floor. (This is especially true on retractable banner stands.) Problem is, you've got people, products, and furnishings in your booth that block the lower part of your signs. Make sure words are placed toward the top of your display. They need to be eye level or higher in order to be the most obvious. The one possible exception is a banner stand placed at the edge of the aisle, but you still run the risk that people may stop and stand in front of the banner, blocking your message.

- **Proof your design before it goes to print.** This goes not only for the actual words, but also the legibility. One good way to test is to print out one word at full size with the chosen background color on an 8.5-by-11-inch sheet of paper, then have someone hold that paper 10-20 feet away. Can you read it, or are you squinting? Another good rule of thumb I use is to look at my complete design as a two-inch thumbnail on my computer. If it's readable that way, it's a pretty safe bet that it will scale up to be readable as a booth-sized graphic. And don't forget to have someone else proof it too ... it's amazing how often your eyes will overlook (or automatically correct for) mistakes in designs you've created.

- **You can be creative without being cluttered or confusing.** Stick with one primary idea per sign or graphic. Big and bold vs. a hodge-podge collage wins every time. And always, always use high-resolution graphics and images so your words are as sharp as possible.

So don't follow the lead of those less-than-readable billboards out there. Study those that are truly eye-catching and memorable ... and pay attention to how easy they are to read.

Where are the signs?

Have you ever been lost? If so, I'm sure you remember the frustration of wandering around looking for a way to wherever it was you were trying to go.

I know I've experienced that feeling. Once I was with a friend in a building where I know my way around very well, but there was an event going on and they were detouring people around the main hall. "No problem," I assured my friend. We asked an employee who pointed and said, "Just go out the east door and around the back of the building."

Easy enough, right? But the problem came when there was no sign indicating where we were supposed to re-enter the building. We went all the way to the end of the sidewalk and ended up at a dead-end fence. Another group was not too far behind us, so together we all began backtracking until someone discovered an unlocked door. When we opened it, we discovered a sign with an arrow ... attached to the inside of the non-glass door!

It's really amazing how many times trade shows and events make this same mistake. It often involves directional signage (like the example above), where attendees start along a path, but end up being forced to make a decision at an unmarked fork somewhere along the way. (One clue: You'll often see a crowd of people with deer-in-the-headlight looks gathering in those areas.) As event planners, it's important to

Signage Types

Banner Stands: Typically tension fabric or vinyl attached to extension poles, often retractable for easy setup and storage; can be more deluxe with backlighting or rotation

Stand-out Header: Attached to the front of the display backwall to make it 'pop'

Hanging: Often tension fabric suspended from the ceiling; typically expensive to install

Cut-Out Lettering: Creates a 3-D effect; best when used for only a few words or just the company name/logo

walk the same path that attendees will, noting each decision point along the way. Every one of those spots needs to have a sign of some kind. If nothing else, at least an arrow pointing straight ahead that says "XYZ Event this way."

A different type of signage mistake is common to exhibitors, like we addressed earlier: too small, too unreadable, or too busy, among other factors. Any of these issues could be easily resolved if exhibitors would remember one simple fact.

Seriously — how much reading do you do when walking the aisles of a trade show? If you're like most people, probably as little as possible while cruising down the aisles. But when you read a sign that grabs your attention, you stop.

Remember, think billboard. Any good billboard has text that is big and bold, with only a few words. The same holds true in the booth. Six or seven word headlines which are clearly focused are much more effective than a whole paragraph. Reduce the noise and clutter.

By following these guidelines and looking at everything from your attendees' viewpoint, one of the biggest challenges at many trade shows and events will now be one of the simplest to correct.

I love the quote I came across in an article about retail signage, which definitely applies to trade shows as well: "Scream less and guide more."

Inside the bonus materials for this chapter:

- Examples of good/bad fonts and color combinations
- Photos of signage types

The Elements of Design

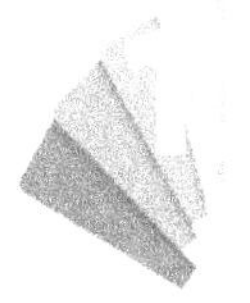

Good design = Form + Function

If you've taken any art classes, you're likely familiar with the basic elements of design. But in case you don't consider yourself an artist, that's okay. You can still benefit from a basic understanding of what those elements are and the role they play in good design. Being familiar with these terms certainly can't hurt when you communicate with your designer!

Line: A mark that connects two points, either straight or curved; varies by length, width, direction and focus (sharp vs. fuzzy); often used to divide content, create emphasis or movement, or draw the eye to a specific part of a design

Shape: Geometric (circle, square, triangle, etc.), organic (leaves, flowers, etc.), or abstract (stylized); defined by boundaries of lines or colors and how they interact; can be positive or negative (the space in between elements — think of the arrow in the FedEx logo)

Color: Can be a background or any element within a design; creates a mood with cool vs. warm colors; the Color Wheel is grouped into primary, secondary, and tertiary/intermediate, which can be combined in various ways; each color takes on different meanings in various cultures (we'll cover color in greater depth in the next chapter)

Texture: Adds depth with tactile or visual interest; real/tactile texture is the actual surface feel of an object that can be touched; visual/implied texture is the illusion created in a two-dimensional photo or graphic that makes it appear soft or hard, rough or smooth

What makes a design great is how skillfully these elements are combined using the principles of harmony, perspective, repetition, rhythm, contrast, balance and scale.

Graphic Design

When choosing someone to design your booth graphics, remember it's important to select a designer who has experience working with trade shows versus simply print or Web projects. A trade show designer will understand how to create large-format, high-resolution graphics for impact on the show floor. Not sure how to find them? Get referrals from other exhibitors, then contact those designers for samples and references.

Design to draw eyes upward, not down to the floor. Keep the focus high so it doesn't get hidden behind people and fixtures in your booth. And don't get text-heavy! Less is more when it comes to words on your display, and don't get too creative with fonts or colors (as you remember from the previous chapter). Instead, choose photos of people using your products (known as lifestyle images), which will attract attention, evoke emotion, and help visitors self-qualify themselves. If you're using stock images, be sure you have all the proper licensing — you don't want to be hit with huge fines or a cease-and-desist order because you skipped this step!

Printing oversized graphics requires very large, high-resolution photos. Don't send your designer a photo you shot on your smartphone!

There are many options for materials and finishes for printing your graphics: fabric, vinyl, backlit panels, and more. Fabric is becoming a popular choice because of its flexibility and affordability to purchase, ship, and set up. It's also easily replaced as needed. The best choice for your exhibit will depend on a number of factors, including the desired texture, look and durability. Be sure you communicate your needs and objectives in very clear language to your designer.

And speaking of how to work with designers ... one of their biggest complaints is clients who say they want something "modern" or "creative." What does that mean? Get specific about your likes and dislikes, but be open to their suggestions. Here are a few other things you will want to convey to your designer:

- Marketing materials and company information (share your corporate branding guide)

- Examples of previous displays used

- Products that will be displayed in the booth

- Date of the first show where you plan to use the display

Once your graphics have been printed, it's important that you care for them so they last for the most number of shows possible. Pay attention to how they're packed for transport — you don't want them to arrive wrinkled or cracked. But if things do go wrong, it's also a good idea to carry copies of your graphics files on a thumb drive, just in case you need to reprint something once you arrive in the show city.

Lighting

Closely tied to your graphics, lighting can be used to convey a mood or reinforce your message. It can focus attention on one particular element within the booth or add drama to the overall space. Make it part of the comprehensive design from the planning stage, not as an afterthought. For example, some lighting will need to be built into the basic structure if it needs rigging or mounting. Of course before you get too far into planning, be sure that your chosen lighting is approved by the show venue (check your show manual).

These days, LEDs (light-emitting diodes) are the go-to lighting technology in exhibits, partly due to the quality of light produced and because there are so many options. You can choose an adjustable-arm style to create a wash of light on your backwall, puck lights to put particular products in the spotlight, or a strip or panel of LEDs for under-shelf highlighting or to create a backlit fabric or vinyl graphic.

Some specialized lighting you may want to consider:

- **Spotlight:** a focused beam used to highlight a product or area

- **Accent:** defines the space or creates depth and dimension

- **Uplighting:** lights under shelves or cabinets to make product displays "glow"

- **Track:** general lighting or spotlights on a truss frame

- **Gobo:** used to project a logo or image, even directional signage (like IKEA's arrows on the floor)

Color temperature plays a big role in lighting. It can range from warm (think traditional incandescent light bulbs) to cool white (clean, bright light), to daylight (tends to have a bluish tint, like the overhead fluorescent bulbs found in some commercial buildings). LEDs typically provide intense, bright white light, but can often be engineered to provide a wide range of accent colors. (Some even come with controllers to change colors while in use.) This can make a big difference depending on what products you're displaying! For example, warm light makes fruit look more attractive, but cool will be more flattering for denim apparel. Changing the lighting color can also make a drastic difference on the appearance of your graphics, so be sure to preview to find the best look.

The lighting you choose can differentiate you from all the other exhibits on the show floor. It can provide a "wow" factor or create a theatrical effect. Use it strategically to focus attention, provide direction, create energy in your booth, or whatever else will best enhance your message and goals.

Flooring

One often-neglected aspect of exhibit design is what's under your feet. Many exhibitors simply rent carpet from the show's general contractor without realizing they're missing an opportunity to customize their look.

Flooring choices go far beyond carpet. There's wood or wood-like, laminate, snap-together floor tiles, artificial turf, and also green options including bamboo, cork, or even flooring made from recycled pop bottles or tires. There are even raised floors, which are common in Europe, but need to be used with caution in the U.S. due to safety and ADA regulations.

Whatever material you choose, it should coordinate with the overall look and feel of your booth. If you have a theme, reinforce that. For example, outdoor themes work well with artificial turf or a bamboo look. Incorporate your brand if it makes sense. Carpet and vinyl can include your logo or other custom images. You can even use multiple colors of carpet or other flooring to create directional paths or zones within a large booth.

No matter what material you decide to use, remember that flooring is more than the surface that shows. Be sure to also include padding underneath (your booth staff will thank you).

People prefer curved lines over straight in architecture and design — perhaps because most lines in nature have curves.

Visual Merchandising

When it comes to product displays, there are an infinite number of options available. Depending on what you want to show off, would it look best on shelves, tables, stands, hanging rods, grids, or something else?

Back to the idea of thinking like retail — what type of look makes sense? Grocery stores have a dizzying array of products, all clustered together by type. High-end designer stores, on the other hand, have more sparse displays that tend to put products in the spotlight. No matter what method you choose, include props that will help to highlight how your product can be used and consider placing small signs alongside items that need a bit of explanation (known in the retail world as "shelf talkers").

Think outside the predictable shelving or grids and make your products appear like a work of art. I remember one year at the HD Expo (the show for designers in the hospitality industry), one chair manufacturer used their island space to create a tiered display with various white chairs on each level. The result looked like a giant wedding cake!

Have massive equipment that costs a fortune to ship and display? Create a scale model of the products. (This also works well for showcasing a venue such as a hotel or attraction.) People are always fascinated by miniatures, plus if you can make the model interactive in some way, they'll spend time exploring in more detail.

Other exhibitors have taken the idea of artwork more literally and actually created the look of a museum or art gallery within their booth. Products are displayed on pedestals or inside ornate frames with museum lighting. At other shows, all kinds of products have been artfully displayed inside a stylish glass reception counter, from bling-encrusted water bottles to fresh oranges. One food company even designed a chilled showcase so they could display rows of their brightly colored yogurt cartons.

Numerous shows have taken a cue from the fashion world. I've seen runway-style fashions featuring all kinds of products:

- Newly-published books carried down a runway by models dressed according to the book's topic. Later that exhibitor had mannequins on display holding the books throughout the rest of the show. (This was a publisher at BookExpo, but could also work with many other types of products.)

- The Pursuing Zero Waste Fashion Show at NPE2015 featured garments designed by students at the Savannah College of Art and Design that were made from recycled or reused plastics. (You'll find a profile of of this show on the **Trade Show Insights** blog.)

- One of my all-time favorites was at HD Expo, where an upholstery fabric exhibitor decided to create runway-style fashions made from their drapery and furniture fabrics, then set up a mini runway of mannequins in their booth. It definitely showed off their inventory in a fun and fresh way!

And talk about a creative way to display products … how about half of an antique truck with hay bales in the middle of a high-tech show? That's exactly what a startup company did one year at CES. To maximize a small space, the front half of the truck was part of the backwall graphic, while the actual truck bed held the product displays. (You'll find a photo in my Exhibit Design Inspiration board on Pinterest.)

Technology

With all the tech tools available these days, it's no wonder exhibitors often go overboard and add too many things just because they can. But just like with all the other elements, it's important to think about what you're trying to achieve, and then incorporate the technology that will get you closer to your goals.

Here are some examples of tools to create an experience attendees can't get back at the office or while sitting on their couch at home:

- **Tablet kiosks:** These are great for interactive games or quizzes, as well as self-serve information stations which provide videos or product details. They can also be used for lead retrieval or onsite attendee surveys. And because they offer so much interaction, they can be programed with custom apps that offer virtual demonstrations or interactive product comparisons.

- **Touch-screen displays:** Like a tablet on steroids, these screens can be scaled up to become an entire wall of the exhibit. Attendees can self-select to view videos or interact with 3-D models of products.

- **Augmented reality (AR):** Used to enhance printed materials by superimposing a virtual object. It uses codes or tags embedded in the print material, which when viewed with a mobile device app creates a composite layer on top of an attendee's physical surroundings. A great example of this is the IKEA catalog that included AR tags so customers could see how a particular piece of furniture would look in their own rooms. On the show floor, this could be used to give virtual tours of how a large piece of equipment works, without having to transport that item to the show.

- **Virtual reality (VR):** While related to AR, this technology actually immerses the user in an artificial simulation. It typically requires viewers to wear a headset or goggles, which creates an alternate reality. Since it came out of the gaming world, it's often used to transport viewers to an active location, like hiking a mountain or flying over the countryside. But it could also be a great tool for virtual site tours or realistic product demonstrations.

- **3-D Printers:** You can have these on hand to print samples, prototypes, or scale models to give to attendees.

- **Projection mapping:** This technology has the ability to transform virtually any object — including a wall of water — into a projection screen without distorting the projected image. You can use it to create interactive graphics or put your product in motion. Examples include transforming a static car on display into a color-changing, scene-shifting movie. Or a humorous miniature chef creating dishes right in front of your eyes on the tabletop. Or how about a larger-than-life fashion show projected onto a wall of water? (Ralph Lauren did that in the middle of Central Park!)

There are so many technology options available that you could explore for your exhibit design — and they're constantly changing! So rather than trying to cover it all here, you'll find updates and cool new tools in the bonus materials.

If reading this chapter has left you feeling overwhelmed, you might benefit from an exhibit brainstorming session, where we spend about 45 minutes on the phone defining your vision and mapping out a solid plan of action for your exhibit design. I love walking exhibitors through the process!

Inside the bonus materials for this chapter:

- Photos and/or links to some of the examples mentioned
- Links to two-part podcast interview with Michelle Bruno on "Event Technology: The Future is Now"
- Audio interview with Katina Rigall Zipay on "Design Trends for Memorable Exhibits"
- More information on using stock photos
- Link to video by Display Supply & Lighting showing a real-world example of creative LED lighting
- Link to a Lighting Color Temperature Chart
- Link to blog post with TS Crew on "The Truth About Trade Show Flooring"
- Links to watch videos of the projection mapping examples

The Power of Color

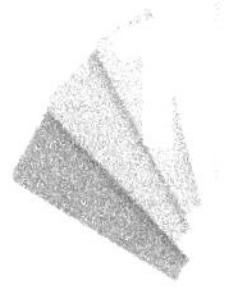

When you think of Coca-Cola, what color do you see? What about McDonald's famous arches? Could you imagine either of these famous icons in, say, green or blue? It just wouldn't have the same effect. (Not to mention the fact that those specific colors are a carefully-protected part of each brand.)

You need to carefully consider color in your trade show booth in the same way. Obviously, if you have legendary corporate colors like the companies above, start there. But if you don't, or if you're wanting to develop something completely different (with only your logo in the corporate color scheme), spend some time evaluating what direction to take.

For example, what mood are you wanting to create? If your focus is on fun, then use brights or primary colors (for a kid-like atmosphere). Want to communicate trust and stability? Go with blues or greens. And if your product is all-natural ... choose an earth-toned color scheme.

The Language of Color

Here are some of the most common messages associated with basic colors to help you decide what will be most effective in your booth (if your audience is in the U.S.). A word of caution: You'll want to carefully research what color messages you're sending to people from other parts of the world.

Red: High-energy, excitement and power (but also signals anger or danger — think Do Not Enter or Stop signs)

Blue: Trust, loyalty and serenity (but can also have an impersonal feel when overdone)

Green: Money and growth, environmental and fresh (but also signifies jealousy)

Yellow: Cheerful, creative and fun (but can be viewed as flighty or irresponsible)

Orange: Confident and friendly (but can also be considered impulsive or aggressive)

Purple: Imaginative, luxurious or royal (but also has a mysterious, moody vibe)

Pink: Happy, playful and sweet (but tends to be perceived as immature or feminine)

Brown: Friendly, conservative and earthy (but can be boring when used alone)

Gray: Reliable and secure (but also gloomy and boring)

Black: Dramatic and classic (but also symbolizes mystery and death)

White: Innocent, pure and clean (but also stark and cold)

Within each color, there are variations ranging from light to dark (values). Adding white to a basic color gives brighter or lighter tints, while adding black creates darker, duller shades.

If you're stuck when it comes to colors, seek inspiration. Look at magazines (outside your industry), restaurants, or interior design books. If all your competitors seem to have similar colors in their displays, then experiment with something completely different. Get a color wheel (available at art supply or craft stores) and consider your competitors' color opposites.

Understanding Color Wheel Basics

Sir Isaac Newton is credited for creating the first circular color diagram back in the 1600s. While the look may have changed dramatically since then, the basic 12-part structure remains:

- Three primary colors (red, yellow, and blue)

- Three secondary colors (green, orange, and purple/violet), which are formed by combining the primary colors

- Six tertiary colors (yellow-orange, red-orange, red-violet, blue-violet, blue-green, and yellow-green), which are formed by mixing a primary color with a secondary color

Color Schemes

Once you understand how the color wheel is arranged, you can begin to combine colors in harmonious color schemes.

- **Monochromatic:** Varying tones of the same color, like light green combined with dark green.

- **Complementary:** Two contrasting colors directly opposite each other on the color wheel, such as blue and orange, or purple and yellow.

- **Analogous:** Any three colors that are side by side on the color wheel, such as orange, red-orange, and red.

- **Triad:** Three colors that are equally spaced on the color wheel, for example yellow-orange, red-violet, and blue-green.

Remember that colors appear different based on the context of what colors are around them. Red will pop against a black background, but blend into an orange one. And against green (red's opposite) ... it creates a vibrating effect! (You'll find color scheme examples in the bonus materials.)

CMYK vs RGB vs Pantone?

If you've ever paid attention to the range of clothing colors hanging in your closet, you've likely noticed that there are endless variations of blues or reds, or even blacks, for that matter. Rarely do two garments purchased at different times match.

It's the same with colors when you're printing materials for your display. Just saying "cranberry" or "crimson" won't necessarily get the red you want. That's why designers use three different color identification systems to pinpoint exactly what shade a particular color will turn out.

RGB

This is the system used for the digital representation of colors on a monitor or digital camera. It stands for red, green and blue. It's not used for printing — so don't give your printer a file created in RGB!

CMYK

The four colors in this system are cyan (blue), magenta, yellow and black. CMYK is used in the four-color printing process (think of the ink tanks in your office printer). All the variations of colors are created using combinations of those four inks. (Except for white, which shows up where the ink is absent, as long as the material you're printing on is white.)

Pantone Matching System

Pantone is the worldwide standard language for color identification, matching, and communication. It's the best choice when a color must be precise — like a corporate logo or product packaging.

The PMS color fan deck contains nearly 2,000 colors with specific ink formulas used to create each one. In addition to a deck for graphic designers and printers, there are also ones created specifically for fabrics, plastics and more.

One important thing to keep in mind: every printer is calibrated slightly differently, so there's no guarantee that the finished product will end up looking exactly the same as the way it prints out on your office printer. There will be variations in the final color result, depending on whether you're printing on fabric, vinyl, or backlit panels. There are also significant differences between the RGB colors on your monitor and a finished print project. So always consult with your designer and/or print shop to get their advice on how to best get the finished look you intended. And if you need something in an exact color, use the Pantone system.

I'm a color junkie. I look forward to the seasonal Pantone color predictions every spring and fall, and take advantage of every color workshop I can attend. I've even studied color forecasting a bit so I can attempt to predict what the color gurus will choose each year. But my advice to exhibitors is that you don't need to be a slave to color trends. (What tends to matter more for exhibit design is which textures are on-trend, such as wood grains, metal finishes, and fabrics.) But it is smart to pay attention to the trends, perhaps more to avoid creating a display that appears dated … unless you're going for that retro look.

Above all, remember that color is a very powerful communicator. If you're a financial company, for example, and you select a bubble-gum pink and purple scheme, you may be trendy, but won't be sending the right message to your audience. Never put fashion ahead of substance.

Inside the bonus materials for this chapter:

- Photos and/or links to some of the case studies mentioned
- More in-depth information and examples of how to use color (including color scheme examples)
- Link to Pantone resources

"You can use an eraser on the drafting table or a sledgehammer on the construction site."

often attributed to Frank Lloyd Wright

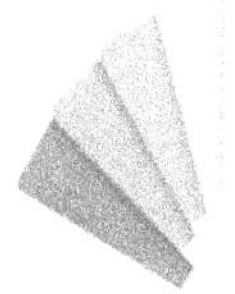

Design with the End in Mind: What's Next?

- Decide which exhibit display type best aligns with your budget and goals.

- Pretend you're an attendee approaching the booth for the first time. What catches your eye, and is it obvious why you should stop at this booth?

- What design elements can you include in your display to attract attention and highlight what makes your company/products special?

“Never confuse motion
with action.”

Benjamin Franklin

Part 6:
The Life Cycle of Exhibits

Once you've developed the creative strategy behind your exhibit design, that's the time to begin the actual process of constructing your booth display, right?

Not so fast! There are still a few more decisions to be made at this stage. First you must determine your budget, including the long-term cost of the exhibit, which we'll explore in chapters 19 and 20.

Just in case that budget isn't quite big enough to accommodate an entirely new booth, don't despair! You don't always have to start from scratch. Sometimes it makes more sense to upgrade your current display or simply switch out certain elements. And sometimes you may even want to rent your exhibit. You'll discover some creative solutions in chapters 21 and 22.

And what if you want to design an environmentally-friendly exhibit? We have that covered in chapter 23.

If you want your booth to last
several years, don't design
it to be too trendy.

Exhibit Design Economics

When establishing your exhibit design budget, there's more to factor in than just the structure and graphics costs. You also need to consider the costs for storage, setup, drayage and shipping that display. Of course there will also be maintenance and/or refurbishing costs over time.

Don't simply look at designing an exhibit as a one-time cost — plan for the lifespan of the booth. A good goal is for it to last three to five years, so factor the cost over the number of shows you plan to exhibit at during that timeframe.

Longer exhibit lifespans also bring up another consideration: How are the materials packaged — will they endure the tests of time and travel? For example, lightweight tension fabric graphics may save a lot on shipping and storage costs, but they also need some special care or else they won't last long.

When you purchase a new exhibit display, always hang onto the setup instructions. In fact, it's a good idea to make copies and keep them in different locations. Add in some detailed diagrams or step-by-step photos. This can save a lot of time and frustration (not to mention labor costs) later!

It's also smart to know how things repack in the cases or crates. Take photos when you receive everything from your exhibit designer (or maybe they'll even include these for you) and keep those inside the case. Number your cases and be sure to save all the necessary packing materials.

Plan Ahead to Save

One smart way to maximize your investment is to plan a design that can be reconfigured for multiple sizes of booth spaces as well as different audiences. This gives you options and makes it easy to adapt on short notice if needed.

When you're working with your exhibit designer, think logistics as well as aesthetics. What technology do you plan to use in your booth (laptops, kiosks, lead retrieval machines, monitors, lighting, etc.)? Plan those electrical needs into the design from the beginning so there's no "oops" moments later. And speaking of electrical ...

Besides basic show labor (installation & dismantle, forklifts, rigging, etc.), there are other exhibit services to keep in mind regarding budget: electrical, cleaning, WiFi, equipment and/or furniture rental, carpet, floral, and more. Always order those services early to take advantage of discounts and avoid paying onsite premiums.

What Do Exhibit Displays Cost?

While there are exhibit display options available in virtually every price range, here are some general guidelines for what you can expect to pay. (These numbers are based on industry research and conversations with exhibit design companies.)

Average custom exhibit: $130-150 per square foot

Average portable exhibit: $300-800 per linear foot (exhibitors tend to spend more per foot for a 30-foot display than a 10-foot display; you can also find options outside this range if you're on a tight budget)

Care & Maintenance of Exhibits

Once you've spent good money on an exhibit display and all the accessories, you'll want to maximize that investment.

Keep a complete inventory of all your cases, crates, and exhibit components. In fact, it's a good idea to do an inventory of all items you plan to take to the show: furniture and fixtures, giveaways, audio/ visual equipment, and more. I've created a Trade Show Asset Inventory checklist to help you with this. You'll find it in the bonus materials for this book.

If you have tension fabric graphics, use caution when handling them during setup and teardown. Be sure your hands are clean (or wear gloves). Also, be careful how you store the fabric to prevent wrinkles from forming. While some fabrics may smooth out on their own, you don't want any surprises the next time you unpack for a show! (But if a few wrinkles do form, you can use a garment steamer during setup to pop them out.)

While you're still at the show, before you pack up, take photos of any damages you notice. This not only documents the damage, but also serves as a reminder to take care of it before the next show rolls around.

In between shows, it's always a good idea to inspect and clean your display. If any fabric panels need cleaning, be sure to pay attention to the care instructions. (Which you kept when you received them, right?)

Right after a show is the time to replace any bulbs, hardware, magnets or other missing parts of your exhibit while it's still fresh on your mind. Be sure all connections function properly and make arrangements to replace any damaged or worn graphics now before you're in crunch time for the next show. It's also a good time to check out the condition of all your shipping cases and padding.

Another good practice is to set up your booth at least once a few weeks or months prior to the next show. This serves as a dress rehearsal to see how everything works and streamlines your setup time, plus it provides a chance to see how the finished display will look. Study it from an attendee's perspective — do you need to pare down a bit because it's too cluttered? You want to discover any issues now while there's still time to course-correct before the next show.

Inside the bonus materials for this chapter:

- Trade Show Assets Inventory worksheet

Trade Show Emergency Kit

Here are a few basic tools to have on hand in your booth for quick, on-the-spot repairs:

Glass cleaner & paper towels	Cleaning supplies
Tape measure	Level
Hook-and-loop fastener strips	Touch-up paint
Tape (packing, duct & carpet)	Scissors
Multi-use screwdriver	Permanent markers
Steamer for fabric graphics	Extra light bulbs

6 Ways to Reinvent Your Exhibit (without spending a fortune)

You know it's time. You're so embarrassed by the way your exhibit looks that you'd rather hide than stand in that booth as the representation of your brand. But you don't have the budget for a whole new exhibit, so what can you possibly do?

There are many ways to refresh a tired old exhibit without starting from scratch. As long as the basic structure of your design is still in good shape, it's not necessary to buy an entirely new display. Here are some options in various price ranges, but all for much less than the whole enchilada.

1. **Update your look with fresh graphics and signage.** Figure out what your message needs to be for the coming year (or for however many shows), then develop a design that can be used multiple times. To get even more bang for your buck, have it printed on fabric. This is not only economical, but also easier and less expensive to ship because it's lightweight.

2. **Change out the furnishings in your booth.** If you have a lounge area or some kind of display cabinets, you might want to consider renting those items so you can justify changing them out more frequently. Or if it fits your style, take a look at IKEA or some other inexpensive furniture option.

3. **Jazz up your lighting.** Sometimes a display looks tired simply because it's not well-lit. If you don't currently use lighting, you might be amazed at how much even something basic like small spotlights on products can do. If you're getting new graphics anyway, see if you can upgrade to a backlit panel that really pops.

4. **Upgrade your tech.** While this may not be the least expensive way to change your look, it definitely makes a big impression. Let's face it — if your booth lacks or has outdated technology, your company will appear backwards as well. But by adding digital signage or a tablet kiosk, you look fresh and "with it."

5. **Improve what's under your feet.** This is a great option to refresh in more ways than one! By upgrading your flooring (including the padding underneath it), you not only improve your look but also the way you and your booth staff will feel after a long day on the show floor.

6. **Not ready to commit? Rent a new look!** If you know you need a major makeover beyond these quick fixes but just don't have the budget, take a look at renting a whole new booth for a show or two. Don't worry — rentals are not the ugly stepchildren of the exhibit world any longer. In fact, you've probably seen a lot of rentals on the show floor and not even recognized them as being rentals. (You'll read more about this in the following chapter.)

So there's no excuse for continuing to use that cobbled-together, tired-looking, has-been display. Once you recognize that you need a fresh look (read on), start taking the steps above to makeover your exhibit.

How to Know When It's Time for a New Display

Let's face it — we all tend to resist change to some degree. Whether it's getting stuck on wardrobe or hairstyle choices (lose the mullet!), or always driving to work the exact same way, we each have tunnel vision when it comes to certain things. And that likely includes your booth display … when did you last update it?

If your answer involves a date from a previous decade (or even worse, last century), that's definitely too long.

One of the most frequent excuses for not updating is lack of budget. But often an update can be as simple as switching out your graphic for a fraction of the cost of an entirely new display. There are also rental options, where you can take a new whole new design for a test run without making a long-term commitment.

So how can you tell if it's time for an update? Here are five telltale clues:

1. **You're seeing signs of age and battle scars on the display.** Packing and unpacking, shipping, and even time spent in storage can all take a toll on exhibit materials. Once the dings and dents (or duct tape) become obvious to not only your staff but also attendees, your company image also has a ding or two in it.

2. **The images in your graphics are definitely outdated, giving the appearance that your company may be as well.**

3. **Your display configuration no longer works for your needs and you're trying to adapt in a way it was never**

intended. This is like trying to fit a square peg into a round hole — you simply can't make a 20-by-30-foot island transform into an inline booth unless it was specifically designed with that type of flexibility.

4. **Your exhibit messaging is no longer working to draw people in.** Like with outdated images, this can often be updated by simply replacing the graphic panels or signage.

5. **The technology (or lack of it) in your booth is sending all the wrong messages.** This is not to say that you have to include all the latest shiny gadgets, but if all the tech elements are obviously from a previous decade, attendees will assume that you can't possibly help them.

Once you admit it's time for a change, don't delay. Start exploring options and get help before you embarrass yourself any further at a future show!

Inside the bonus materials for this chapter:

- Time to Update checklist
- Link to the webinar replay, "Reinvent Your Trade Show"

Should You Rent Your Next Exhibit?

Sometimes it doesn't make sense to buy an entirely new exhibit display. Perhaps you decide to exhibit at a new show and need a different size booth than usual, or maybe you simply want to test out a fresh design.

Before buying a new display, consider how long or how often you plan to use it. Then calculate your cost per show. Factor in some of the "hidden costs" of ownership, which include: installation and dismantle (I&D) expenses (how much labor is required to set it up), shipping (weight and bulk), storage, and costs for cleaning and refurbishing. These can total 20 percent or more of the original exhibit cost … per year! So what can you do?

Enter exhibit rentals. And no, they're no longer fuddy-duddy, boring flat walls where the only customization is your graphic swapped in for those the last client used. These days, rentals are stylish, curved designs that give the appearance of a custom exhibit. You can also rent accessories like workstations and tablet kiosks as well.

With renting, you're not committed to one specific look and can change things up for each show. It also allows you to spend more on the graphics and signage instead of hardware, and you don't have to worry about storage costs. Your installation and dismantle costs may even be included with the rental. On the other hand, buying a new exhibit means you can totally customize the functionality and materials used, but you're locked into the same look for a longer period of time.

Renting makes a lot more sense than buying when you only plan to use the booth once, or if you have trouble committing to a particular design. Try it out first! It's also a smart option for those times when you have two shows that overlap, or if you decide last-minute to participate in a new show, because renting typically runs about one-third the cost of buying a new exhibit.

You have the ability to mix and match elements or try out new materials without any long-term commitment. And just in case you do like what you try, ask if there's a rent-to-own option.

Ask a few other questions too: Do they rent audio/visual, lighting, and other tech items also? And who is responsible for all the transportation and maintenance issues?

So how do you know whether to rent or buy your next booth? If you have a one-time scheduling conflict or need a special booth size for a certain show, renting is a good alternative. Also, if you want to test out a new design or your company is going through an "image transition," you should opt to rent instead of buying a booth you may not use again. But if you find yourself renting more than three or four times a year, it might be to your advantage to go ahead and buy a new display.

*(Portions of this chapter excerpted from **Build a Better Trade Show Image** © 2002 by Marlys Arnold.)*

Inside the bonus materials for this chapter:

- Rent vs. Buy worksheet
- Link to the *Pinpoint Your Exhibit Savings Solution* white paper

How Green is Your Exhibit?

Perhaps you've never thought about how much impact a trade show can have on the environment. Or maybe you're trying to do your part by recycling your leftover literature and other materials. But there is so much more to it than that. Here are just a few of the options available to exhibitors today.

Display materials

What is your display made out of? Environmentally-friendly design options include bamboo, cork, and recycled plastics. If traditional wood is a must, look for either composite or reclaimed lumber alternatives. Frames can also be designed with recycled (or recyclable) metals, such as aluminum. (One company who is focused on creating sustainable exhibits is Eco-Systems. You can check out that podcast interview in the bonus materials.)

Graphics

Use soy-based ink and print on fabric rather than vinyl. Choose designs that can be used at multiple shows. And when you do retire them, most graphic panels can be recycled (as can many other display materials).

Flooring

Consider using floor coverings made of recycled tires or cork. Not only are they eco-smart (and stylish), but they could be more comfortable as well. If you really want carpet, look for either sisal or recycled carpet.

Lighting

How energy-efficient is your lighting system? And how many lights do you really need? Today's exhibit halls are often bright enough that you don't need much additional light except to spotlight products or create atmosphere. To accomplish that, consider either fluorescent bulbs or LEDs.

Cases

These are also now available in recycled plastic, which provide just as much protection for your display as any other case.

Literature & giveaways

Here you have two choices: cut back on the amount you bring, or recycle (vs. discard) your excess. In addition, be careful who you give items to ... if they're not going to be genuine prospects, your materials may wind up in the nearest trashcan. Think about your audience and give them items that will either be functional or at the very least whimsical and taken home to share with friends.

Don't worry about revamping your entire exhibit overnight. Instead, look to replace one element at a time. At the very least, become aware about how your next trade show might affect the environment and look for ways to make a difference.

Inside the bonus materials for this chapter:

- Links to podcast interviews on green exhibiting
- Link to the Eco-Systems Green Guide

The Life Cycle of Exhibits: What's Next?

- Do the math: What will be the long-term costs of your exhibit?

- If you don't plan to start over (or just plain can't right now, what can you do to refresh your existing exhibit display?

- What green elements can you add to your exhibit design?

"The future depends
on what you do today."

Mahatma Gandhi

Conclusion: Put Your Best Booth Forward

This isn't the end. Not by any means! Your strategic exhibit plan will continue to evolve as your message, audience, trends, and technology change.

Sometimes you may discover that your exhibit design is no longer working. At that point it's time to evaluate what needs to be done to improve before the next show. But that doesn't mean you have to start from scratch. Inside these pages, you have the tools to review which aspects need to change, along with the steps for to how to proceed.

Don't try to follow every example in this book — choose those that align the best with your situation and message, then brainstorm how to use these ideas to make your exhibit stand out from the crowd on the show floor.

Always remember to begin with your goals and budget, then develop your overall exhibit marketing strategy before launching into the actual design process. And keep in mind that no two companies are alike, so there's no one "right" blueprint to follow.

As you've seen in previous chapters, successful exhibiting requires a mix of creativity and strategic planning. Don't get so bogged down in the logistics and checklists that you forget to leave room for the personality and fun in your exhibits.

One other key to success is to partner with industry suppliers that are a good fit for you. That may mean finding a new exhibit designer or technology provider. Or perhaps you want someone to walk through the decision-making process with you before you even contact a designer. If so, please feel free to reach out — I'm happy to help.

Resources

Exhibit Designers & Builders

Classic Exhibits

866-652-2100

www.classicexhibits.com

Design and manufacturing plus exhibit rentals; sells through over 175 distributors across the U.S.

Condit

800-541-6308

www.condit.com

Specializes in custom exhibits; located in Denver, CO

Display Supply & Lighting Inc.

800-468-1488

www.dslgroup.com

Source for lighting and supplies, as well as installation and onsite programming services

Duo Display

877-593-7500

www.duodisplay.com/us/home

Display manufacturer that sells exclusively through an international dealer network

Exhibit Associates Inc.

816-474-5333

www.exhibitassociates.com

Full-service exhibit design, fabrication and installation company located in the Kansas City area

Eco-Systems Sustainable Exhibits

866-463-2611

www.ecosystemsdisplays.com

Designs eco-friendly displays; sells through a distributor network

Exhibit Edge

800-914-5750

www.exhibitedge.com

Full-service exhibit company in the Washington, DC area providing exhibit design and fabrication, as well as storage, labor and transportation

Exhibit Works

734-525-9010

www.ewiworldwide.com

Designs & builds exhibits; a division of EWI Worldwide, a full-service creative services company

Falcon Perspectives, Inc.

718-706-9168

www.falconperspectives.com

Exhibit designer and builder located in New York

Kubik

877-252-2818

www.thinkubik.com

Designs, fabricates, installs and manages exhibits around the world

Lucarelli Designs & Displays, Inc.

866-720-EXPO

www.lddinc.com

Exhibit builder specializing in the integration of lighting systems, audio/visual systems, special effects, theatrical and multimedia

Lynch Exhibits

609-387-1600

www.lynchexhibits.com

Exhibit builder specializing in interactive media, located in NJ

Roundhouse

503-287-0398

www.roundhouseagency.com

Independent, full-service creative agency located in Portland, OR

Steelhead Productions
702-405-0190
www.steelheadproductions.com
Exhibit design and rental company located in Las Vegas

The Tradeshow Network Marketing Group
877-730-5300
www.thetradeshownetwork.com
Full-service exhibit company based in Chicago; provides design, fabrication and rentals, as well as installation, shipping, storage and management of exhibit properties

Other Exhibit Industry Resources

ASCAP
www.ascap.com
Music licensing service

BMI
www.bmi.com
Music licensing service

Center for Exhibition Industry Research (CEIR)
972-687-9242
www.ceir.org
Membership-based organization that provides research reports to help exhibitors be more effective; contact to purchase the reports mentioned in this book

Cort Trade Show Furnishings
888-CORT-YES
www.corttradeshow.com
Furniture rental for trade shows and events (typically ordered through the show's general contractor)

Exhibit City News
www.exhibitcitynews.com
Trade show industry monthly newspaper

Experiential Designers & Producers Association (EDPA)

203-557-6231

www.edpa.com

Members design, produce and service exhibits and experiential environments for trade shows, corporate, museums, retailers, and more

Exhibitor Appointed Contractor Association (EACA)

541-317-8768

www.eaca.com

Members provide services to exhibitors on the show floor including I&D labor, exhibit transportation, carpet/flooring, furniture, computer rental, and more (offers a choice beyond using the show's general contractor for these services)

EXHIBITOR

www.exhibitoronline.com

Publishes a monthly magazine and produces the annual **EXHIBITOR***LIVE conference and trade show*

Healthcare Convention & Exhibitors Association (HCEA)

703-935-1961

www.hcea.org

Association for exhibitors, show organizers, and industry suppliers involved in healthcare conventions and exhibitions

Pantone

866-PANTONE

www.pantone.com

Global authority on color with resources including color fan decks, reports, seasonal forecasts, and more

Trade Show Insights blog/podcast

www.tradeshowinsights.com

News, tips and tools to improve your exhibit results

TS Crew

800-451-0716

www.tscrew.com

Trade show labor and project management for installing and dismantling exhibits on the show floor

Trade Show News Network (TSNN)
www.tsnn.com
Online news resource for the exhibition industry; maintains an event database listing more than 25,000 trade shows, exhibitions, public events, and conferences around the world, plus supplier and venue listings

Recommended Reading

Build a Better Trade Show Image by Marlys K. Arnold, Tiffany Harbor Productions, 2002

Pantone Guide to Communicating with Color by Leatrice Eiseman, Grafix Press, 2000

Telling Ain't Training by Harold D. Stolovitch and Erica J. Keeps, ASTD Press, 2011 (2nd Edition)

The Experience Economy: Work is Theatre & Every Business a Stage by Joseph Pine and James Gilmore, Harvard Business School Press, 1999

Trade Show Terms to Know

Types of Shows

Association show: a show that is held for members of a particular association, often in conjunction with the annual convention

Public/Consumer show: a show that is open to the general public

Trade/Industry show: a show that is open only to qualified members of a specific industry; the term "trade show" is loosely applied to describe all types of exhibitions

Basic Terms

Badge scanner: device used to read the attendees' badges, typically contracted by show management; data can be saved electronically or printed out

Bill of lading: document serving as contract between a shipper and a transportation company that outlines how and where freight will be moved

Drayage: transporting your materials from the loading dock to the booth, storing crates during the show, and getting it all back to the dock after the show

Exhibitor Appointed Contractor (EAC): company selected by an individual exhibitor to provide specific show services; must be approved by show management

General Service Contractor (GSC): company designated by show management to provide all labor and services for exhibitors at the show

I&D: installation and dismantle (set-up and tear-down) of the booth; provided by an appointed contractor

Lead cards: forms used to collect demographic and qualifying data on attendees who visit the booth

Overtime rates: higher rates paid to show labor for setup, drayage, etc. that fall outside the usual Monday-to-Friday daytime hours; some locations charge double time on Sunday and holidays

Pipe & Drape: the tubed framework covered with fabric drapes to create the divider back and side walls at a trade show

Refurbishment: repairing damages and refinishing display surfaces and graphics to extend the exhibit's lifespan

ROI: return on investment; calculating how much business was generated compared to the amount of money spent on the exhibit

Sales cycle: the process that begins with a basic lead and ends with that lead becoming a customer

Show labor: skilled contractors who perform services at a convention center or other show venue; often union employees

Stand: the term for "booth" in Europe

Display Terms

Backwall: a drape or panel along the back of a linear booth

Custom exhibit: a unique display built especially for a specific exhibitor

Double-decker: a two-story booth; subject to special structural regulations

Graphic: elements such as logos, art or photos that enhance a display

Hardwall: a display built of wood or other solid elements as opposed to fabric or flexible panels

Modular: an exhibit made up of interchangeable elements or panels

Portable/pop-up: lightweight units with collapsible frames

Silicone Edge Graphics (SEG): tension fabric graphic panels with a thin silicone strip sewn in which is inserted into special grooves on a frame to pull the fabric taut and hide the frame; often used with backlit panels

Table top: a portable display that fits on top of a table

Booth Space Types

Corner booth: booth at the end of a row bordered by at least two aisles; allows for more flexibility in booth design than an in-line booth

End Cap/Peninsula: booth with an aisle on three sides

Island: freestanding booth with aisles on all four sides; incorporates at least four standard booth spaces

Inline/Linear: standard booth in the middle of a row of booths with aisle access only across the front

Perimeter booth: booth located along the outer wall of the exhibit hall (often the maximum backwall height is higher for these booths, since this would not interfere with any other booths)

Index

Acknowledgements

Exhibit Design That Works is the result of countless interactions and experiences, both on trade show floors and off. Thanks first of all to my mentors and coaches, who have been an integral part of my growth as both an entrepreneur and a writer. Everything you've done to support me is appreciated!

A special thank-you to all who served as examples throughout this book — you rock! I get excited every time I see exhibitors who "get it" and go the extra mile to make their display not only memorable, but also sharable.

I'm also grateful to the group of people who agreed to be my beta readers and sent valuable feedback. Thank you Liz Besser, Dana Doody, Kelly Galea, Bev Gray, Don Jalbert, Karin Roberts, Ruth Scherrer, and Matt Wish. Thanks also to my proofreaders, Leanna Brunner and Wynona Haun (aka Mom).

And finally, thanks to Katina Rigall Zipay, who wrote the foreword for this book. Your designs provide constant inspiration for exhibitors in all kinds of markets.

About the Author

As an exhibit marketing strategist, Marlys Arnold combines image expertise and real-world marketing experience with a passion for trade shows. She's not only been an exhibitor, but also the organizer of several expos and events. This unique perspective of the industry allows her to share new insights with both beginning and experienced exhibitors, teaching how to create experiential exhibits that produce significantly higher numbers of qualified leads without busting a company's budget.

She has led workshops for thousands of exhibitors at all types of events ranging from local consumer expos to some of the largest trade shows in the U.S. Her articles have appeared in trade show industry magazines and business publications, and she's been interviewed on both traditional and online broadcasts.

Marlys enjoys being an educator and advocate for exhibit marketers' success and assisting with their trade show makeovers. She writes the **TradeShowTips Online** e-zine, hosts the ***Trade Show Insights*** blog/podcast, and is the author of ***Build a Better Trade Show Image*** and the ***ExhibitorEd Success System***. She's also the founder of the Exhibit Marketers Café, an online education community, and is a member of the International Association of Exhibitions & Events (IAEE).

For more information, or to purchase bulk copies of this book for your customers or organization, contact:

Marlys K. Arnold, ImageSpecialist
PO Box 901808
Kansas City, MO 64190
816-746-7888
www.tradeshowinsights.com
On Facebook & Twitter: @ImageSpecialist

Want more?

There's no way this book can teach everything there is to know about designing an effective trade show exhibit. While it does provide the fundamentals, perhaps you feel like you need more assistance. If so, here are some options for you.

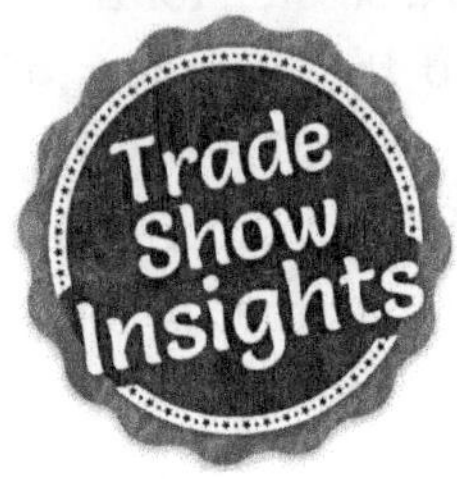

Trade Show Insights blog/podcast

This blog-and-podcast combo hosted by Marlys Arnold features exhibit industry topics and podcast interviews with leading industry professionals. You'll find it at www.TradeShowInsights.com.

ExhibitorEd Success System

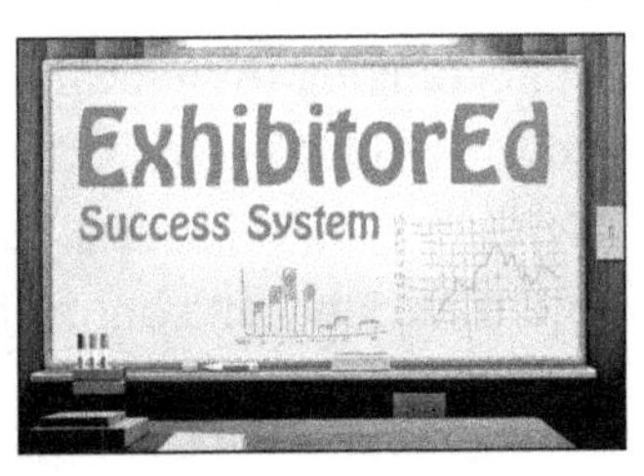

ExhibitorEd is a compilation of tips and tools which includes six self-study modules with accompanying workbooks, each designed to enhance the return on your exhibiting experience. You'll also receive a Second Opinion Certificate, which entitles you to a basic critique of either your booth design or promotions.

Consulting & Exhibitor Training

Want a customized plan to create more buzz, get more qualified leads, and improve ROI from your exhibit marketing strategy? Go beyond basic information with personalized advice and accountability to turn ideas into action. Team up with Marlys to transform your exhibit marketing so you attract more qualified leads and ultimately more sales. (No cookie-cutter solutions here!)

Learn more at: www.ExhibitMarketersCafe.com

Other books by Marlys:

Build a Better Trade Show Image

Was your last trade show exhibit as successful as you had hoped ... or is there still room for improvement? It doesn't matter if you're headed to your first trade show or your 51st — there are steps you might be missing that can make you more successful. This book is filled with tips and proven examples that can jump-start your next exhibiting experience.

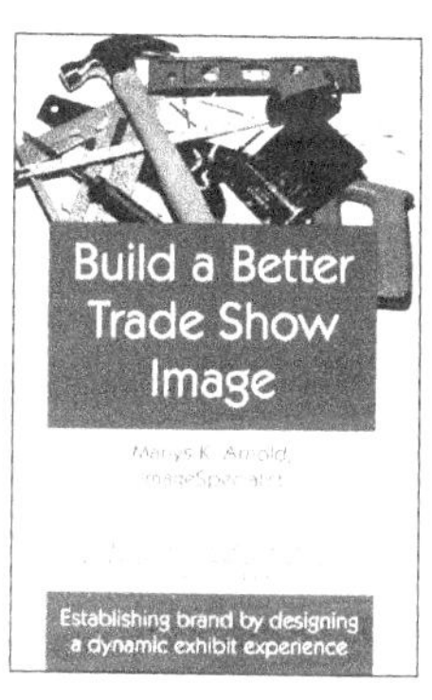

You will discover how to:

- Research shows and set realistic goals for exhibiting
- Make your exhibit stand out with a unique theme or design
- Train staffers so they are able to gather the most qualified leads
- Create a buzz about your company before the show starts
- Unlock the potential in the leads you gather
- Expand your possibilities by implementing non-traditional techniques

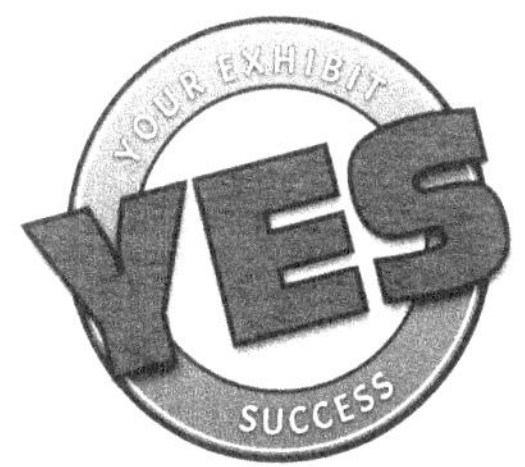

Watch for more books in the *YES: Your Exhibit Success* series on these topics:

Booth Staffing

Marketing & Promotions